WHERE IS GOD AT WORK?

William Morris

MONARCH
BOOKS
Oxford UK, and Grand Rapids, USA

Published by Monarch Books
an imprint of
Lion Hudson plc
Wilkinson House, Jordan Hill Road,
Oxford OX2 8DR, England
Email: monarch@lionhudson.com
www.lionhudson.com/monarch

ISBN 978 0 85721 628 1
e-ISBN 978 0 85721 629 8

First edition 2015

Acknowledgments
Scripture quotations taken from Scripture quotations marked ESV are from The
Holy Bible, English Standard Version® (ESV®) copyright © 2001 by Crossway, a
publishing ministry of Good News Publishers. All rights reserved.
Scripture quotations marked KJV are from The Authorized (King James) Version.
Rights in the Authorized Version are vested in the Crown. Reproduced by
permission of the Crown's patentee, Cambridge University Press.
Scripture quotations marked NIV taken from the Holy Bible, New International
Version Anglicised. Copyright © 1979, 1984, 2011 Biblica, formerly International
Bible Society. Used by permission of Hodder & Stoughton Ltd, an Hachette
UK company. All rights reserved. "NIV" is a registered trademark of Biblica. UK
trademark number 1448790.
Scripture quotations marked NRSV are from The New Revised Standard Version of
the Bible copyright © 1989 by the Division of Christian Education of the National
Council of Churches in the USA. Used by permission. All rights reserved.

A catalogue record for this book is available from the British Library

Printed and bound in the UK, March 2015, LH26

"This book is full of carefully crafted practical wisdom, born of long experience in the workplace and deep reflection on the riches of Christian theology and spirituality."

Revd Dr Graham Tomlin, Dean, St Mellitus College

"In this book Will Morris has married astute and sympathetic observation of the workplace with a deep and lively Christian intelligence. The result is as clear and useful as a how-to manual, but fresher, sharper, and wiser. It's really good."

Nigel Biggar, Regius Professor of Moral and Pastoral Theology, and Director of the McDonald Centre for Theology, Ethics, and Public Life, at the University of Oxford

"A refreshingly honest illustration of workplace challenges. Morris fluently combines wit, positivity and lessons in which our business lives can coexist with our faith and morals."

John Cridland CBE, Director General of the CBI

"This warm, measured, generous book not only offers a wealth of helpful biblical insight into the contemporary office world but above all reminds, inspires, encourages us to work for the God of surprises in the confident and expectant, but never triumphalistic, trust that there is no workplace, no situation, no challenge beyond His concern or kingdom touch."

Mark Greene, London Institute for Contemporary Christianity

"Will Morris writes like he lives: with economy, understatement, humour, integrity, and a good deal of mischief. If his subject was straightforward, others would have dealt with it thoroughly and well, and it would be off the desk. They haven't; and it isn't: and that's why we are immensely in Will Morris' debt that he has given us an example to follow, a vocation to pursue, and a word to enjoy."

Dr Samuel Wells, Vicar of St Martin-in-the-Fields, London, and Visiting Professor of Christian Ethics at King's College London

"When I was a Treasury minister, Will Morris was an exceptionally thoughtful and helpful lobbyist. Now he is ordained, too. His exceptionally thoughtful and helpful book explains how paid work can be part of a life intended to honour Christ."

Rt Hon. Stephen Timms, Shadow Minister for Employment and Labour Party Faith Envoy

"Christian reflection on the world of work and the challenges it poses has regularly suffered from one or other, and occasionally both, of two problems – it is often written by those who are fundamentally suspicious of business in its various forms, and not necessarily well informed about the realities of the workplace. Will Morris speaks and writes with the authority of someone who knows the life of the modern business office from the inside, and who approaches work as something in which Christians may find a vocation. As such, he offers invaluable wisdom and encouragement to those who are seeking to discern Christian meaning and responsibility in their life at work."

Dr Michael Banner, Dean and Fellow of Trinity College, Cambridge

"I do not always agree with Will Morris but on a fundamental issue we are in total agreement; you either take your faith to work with you or you're not putting it to work. This book challenges on that issue in innovative ways and I recommend it."

Richard Murphy, Tax Justice Campaigner

"Everyone who has prayed about their work will appreciate how Will Morris brings out God's creation in every aspect of the workplace, and shows how we can participate in that creation through the daily challenges, dilemmas, frustrations, pains and joys."

Dave Hartnett, Blueprint for Better Business and former Permanent Secretary for Tax, HMRC

Will Morris blogs at whereisgodatwork.org

To Michelle,
without whom nothing would happen, and with
whom everything does. With all my love.

Contents

Part III: Where is God at Work in the Bible?

Acknowledgments

I owe thanks to many people...

Thanks to my colleagues at GE, who have been so supportive of a priest in their midst. Among a crowd of remarkable people, I do want to mention just one in particular: John Samuels, my former boss, who gave me the time and space (and encouragement) I needed to start and complete my ordination training, all the while never questioning my commitment to my day job.

Thanks to my ministry team colleagues and to the congregations of St Martin-in-the-Fields who have also been so supportive and tolerant of a tax lawyer in their midst. Particular thanks go to the faithful Thursday lunchtime group who listened and commented on these chapters when they were first given as talks.

Thanks to Mark Greene who, as the author of *Thank God it's Monday*, is pure inspiration, and generously gave of his time when I was trying to find my way. And to Ed Newell (then at St Paul's) who came and gave the fateful evening lecture mentioned on page 21.

Thanks to four remarkable priests, without whom I would not be where I am (and, in some respects, who I am) today. Robert Atwell, friend and mentor for over thirty years, who persuaded me (correctly) in my twenties not to become a priest, and in my forties (correctly, I hope!) to become one. Nick Holtam, who brought me into St Martin's, gave me a platform on which to work on faith and work issues, and was an inspirational training incumbent. Robert Wiggs, my spiritual director, who tugs and pulls and asks difficult questions out of love that open new possibilities every time we speak. And Sam Wells, who encouraged me to give the talks, and then to try to turn them into a book – but, more importantly, who inspires me through personal conversation and through brilliant preaching and writing, constantly to ask, "Where is Jesus Christ in this?"

Thanks to Andrew Hodder-Williams, Tony Collins, and Jenny Ward at Monarch for their confidence in me, and for shepherding a novice through the publishing process. And thanks to Graham Tomlin for making the connection. I hope all that confidence is repaid!

Thanks to Pat Brown, Marlin Risinger, and James Johnston who read this as fellow workers and offered many helpful suggestions.

And, finally, my most enduring thanks to my family. To my father, always my gold standard for steady, un-showy, faithful, middle-of-the-road Anglicanism, integrated into professional and personal life. And to my mother, who occasionally finds this all a little strange, but always offers unconditional support. To Alex, Julia, and Kat who deal very tolerantly with a father who often seems more absent than present – and who threatens constant embarrassment (in or out of a clerical shirt). And, last but first, to my wife Michelle, also the dedicatee, who quite simply keeps the whole show on the road.

Foreword

Will Morris is a missionary. Once a missionary had khaki shorts, dodgy sandals, a missing space where a sense of humour should be, and a tendency to talk about being on furlough and to complain about how much choice there is in the shops and how much water we waste. Then a misjsionary became someone who put extra syllables in the word Jesus, filled stadiums with crowds, spoke of how God filled the hole in your life, and invited people forward to collect literature.

Will Morris is a different kind of missionary. As the Father sent the Son to be with us, full of grace and truth, and as the Father and the Son sent the Spirit to empower us, with energy of wind and words of fire, so God has sent Will Morris to be with and empower people to live the gospel in work as well as in church, amid P45s as well as amid leather-bound Bibles, within health and safety regimes as well as within four spiritual laws.

Will Morris is also a priest. A priest speaks to the people on behalf of God and to God on behalf of the people. Will certainly does that – never more so than in this book. But as a priest-missionary Will addresses those at work on behalf of the church and addresses the church on behalf of those at work. That's what makes this book unique. Will speaks with equal authority when asking what on earth a person in the workplace is supposed to make of the ridiculous demands of this parable, as when asking what in heaven God's people are to do when faced with the apparently acceptable conventions of an exploitative company.

It is this toing and froing that has constituted Will's life these last few years. And, rather than give us an account of his extraordinary life – and believe me, he's been on more planes and in more boardrooms and at more lunchtime communions than you could care to imagine – he much more humbly offers us the fruits of his reflections on Scripture, work, and what it means to put the two together and trust that from them will emerge holiness.

Will Morris writes like he lives: with economy, understatement, humour, integrity, and a good deal of mischief. If his subject was straightforward, others would have dealt with it thoroughly and well, and it would be off the desk. They haven't, and it isn't; and that's why we are immensely in Will Morris' debt that he has given us an example to follow, a vocation to pursue, and a word to enjoy.

Revd Dr Samuel Wells
Vicar of St Martin-in-the-Fields, London, and Visiting Professor of Christian Ethics at King's College London

Introduction

I am a priest. I am a tax lawyer. As a priest, I celebrate the Eucharist, I preach, I lay on hands and anoint with oil, I listen, I wear a clerical shirt and "dog collar" (sometimes), and I go to parish coffee hours. I am part of the team at St Martin-in-the-Fields, the "church of the ever open door" and a pioneer in social care and outreach to the homeless. As a tax lawyer, I work on international tax policy, I travel globally, I meet with politicians and civil servants, and I chair business groups that interact with national, regional, and international organizations. I am part of the team at GE (General Electric), one of the largest companies in the world. My job is to ensure that GE in particular, and business in general, are not adversely affected by changes to tax law, and that taxes on business remain as low as possible.

To many people there's something very strange about that pairing, perhaps even mutually exclusive. Some ask: How can you be a priest at the weekends and a tax lawyer during the week? Others ask: Does what you do at the weekends make you feel better about/absolve you from what you do during the week? The presumption that I can only live a compartmentalized life, doing good in one area and something (presumably) less good in another, is very strong. But it's wrong. There is a missing conjunction. I am a priest **and** a tax lawyer, both of them, all the time – at work, away from work, during the week, on Sundays. I am both, and if I am to live the one life that I have "well" (an adverb that needs more unpacking than I can do here), then I have to hold the two in tension, in balance, in my one life.

In other contexts this statement would not be regarded as remarkable. I am husband, father, son, and brother; lover of history; episodic Liverpool FC supporter; avid, if occasional, theatregoer – and on and on. No one would argue for strict compartmentalization between those areas. Of course, one may get more attention at any one moment, but they are all part of a single life. When it comes to God and work, however, there is a perceived disconnect, an assumption that somehow the two don't, can't, go together (except, perhaps, in the caring professions). There are exceptions to this view, especially in the Evangelical community, but it is generally pervasive. God = good; work for profit = less good/bad.

Yet, as I explore in the opening chapters, if we believe in God, then I think we have to believe in a Creator God. God didn't just happen along after the event; God worked, and that work was important to God. And however we understand the creation story, working – whether growing crops, raising livestock, building temples, manufacturing goods, or providing services – is an integral part of living as a human being. Although worship and prayer and contemplation are also fundamental to our lives as children of God, it is an "also". God cares about work and is as present there as in church or anywhere else – and to say He doesn't care and isn't there does Him a disservice. It does us an even bigger disservice, however, because we miss the opportunity for a totally different level of fulfilment than if we simply "work to live" without any sense of where God might be in that work.

But there's even more to it than God merely being interested in work. God did not simply set the world going, and then install us as caretakers or janitors. Something happened to the world ("the fall", imperfection, whatever), with the result that if the first act of God was creation of the world, then the subsequent acts are the healing and redemption of that world (and its inhabitants). So our opportunity to work with God (the dynamic trio of Father, Son, and Holy Spirit) is not just in making things for the sake of making things, but making things and providing services that can help the healing of creation – and of God's people. In other words, all in all, work might be pretty important.

Now, I am the last person in the world to argue that every workplace is great, and that work is always fulfilling. But, because it is important to God, it has the potential to be fulfilling. It is that potential that interests me, because it opens up so many possibilities – for bettering our own lives, and not just ours, of course, but also those of others. What I try to explore in this book is how, because of the importance of work to God, if we exercise our imagination, if we leave ourselves open to possibilities, we may find God at work – even in the form of our boss, our annoying colleagues, or the arrival of a P45 (US: pink slip). God may also be present in the dilemmas that occur at work: if we're asked to work harder and harder, asked to lie, tempted to do something bad. Finally, by looking at the workplace through the prism of a single parable, but from several different angles, we may also glimpse through Scripture where God may be at work.

There's probably another book on maintaining the appropriate balance (creative tension, perhaps) between being a priest and a tax lawyer – although I begin to sketch out an answer based on Richard Rohr's idea of "living on the edge of the inside" – but at its heart is the idea, belief, understanding, that work is important to God, and yet it also poses real challenges to us as humans. Being aware of the possibility of God in the workplace is both a significant challenge (you can't hide...) and an enormous comfort (I can work with God here, too). Living and working in an ambiguous place – including the moral grey zone of tax – may not be comfortable, nor seem that enticing. But it is where most of us are, and trying to see what the godly potential might be, rather than trying to shut it off from the "good" (= church) part of our lives, is our challenge as working Christians.

I hope that what follows may enable you to glimpse where God might be with you during the day at work, and how you may work with God. It can be a surprise, but if you keep eyes, ears, and mind open then, perhaps, like Jacob, you will also find yourself saying, "Surely the Lord is in this place – and I did not know it!" (Genesis 28:16 NRSV).

PART I

Where is God at Work?

1

The Workplace

Genesis 28:11–17 (NRSV)

He came to a certain place and stayed there for the night, because the sun had set. Taking one of the stones of the place, he put it under his head and lay down in that place. And he dreamed that there was a ladder set up on the earth, the top of it reaching to heaven; and the angels of God were ascending and descending on it. And the Lord stood beside him and said, "I am the Lord, the God of Abraham your father and the God of Isaac; the land on which you lie I will give to you and to your offspring; and your offspring shall be like the dust of the earth, and you shall spread abroad to the west and to the east and to the north and to the south; and all the families of the earth shall be blessed in you and in your offspring. Know that I am with you and will keep you wherever you go, and will bring you back to this land; for I will not leave you until I have done what I have promised you." Then Jacob woke from his sleep and said, "Surely the Lord is in this place – and I did not know it!" And he was afraid, and said, "How awesome is this place! This is none other than the house of God, and this is the gate of heaven."

If you were asked to spot the odd one out in the following pairs – salt and pepper, bread and butter, knife and fork, God and workplace – the answer is obviously "God and workplace". The two are so far from being a complementary pair that the dissonance is hardly even worth noting. It's so unremarkable that we accept it without thinking and move on. But perhaps we should pause a moment, consider it more, and dig down a little. Why are they so obviously incompatible? Why are "God" and "workplace" such clear opposites in our minds?

Of course, we can complain that it's the fault of secularism in the modern workplace that squeezes out all references to, and thoughts of, God. About businesses so fearful of favouring anyone – including in relation to religion – that they end up disadvantaging everyone. God has been banished from the public square, we can tell ourselves. But, in fact, I think that most of the problem lies not with secularism, but with us as Christians. Beliefs, issues, come at us from two directions, combining to form an impenetrable barrier – in our minds – between God and our workplace.

One set of issues arise from that significant part of the institutional church that, whatever it says, really only believes that God exists in church, on a Sunday morning, preferably with liturgy and hymns. On this view we can only meet God in a building with an altar, a cross, and pews, and at a certain time. For all the talk of café churches and weekday house groups, our Christian culture, our upbringing (and some of our church leaders) all make us consciously or unconsciously feel, believe, that God is only – or, at the very least, is especially – present in church, on the sabbath.

The other set of issues come from an equally deeply held belief by many Christians that God and religious activity are "good" and "pure", while office work or anything done for a salary (and especially for profit) is, at the very least, inferior, probably slightly grubby, or possibly even just plain dirty. And if that's the case, then how on earth can God be there in that?

Both of these ideas are deeply rooted in Western culture.

And yet countless millions of people in the UK and elsewhere spend eight or more hours in workplaces every day. What is the church saying to them? God doesn't love you? God doesn't care? You're wasting your time and skills doing this? That may not be what the church thinks it's saying, but that's sometimes very much what it sounds like. And then the church wonders why these people (now the significant majority) think Christians are weird; wonders why they don't want to come to church, and why they don't think that religion has anything to say to them or wants anything to do with them.

I spent the first year of my training to be a priest wondering what on earth I was doing. I was really there only because no one in the process of selection and training had said "no". There was a vague, nagging feeling that God was somehow driving (dragging?) me forward, but there had been no clear light shining on the road, no fixed plan. Then, one evening, someone came to teach a class on "faith and the workplace". Suddenly I realized what it was that I was doing, and why I was doing it.

I had always known that I was going to carry on with my secular ("day") job after ordination – but perhaps switch from the slightly grubbier, commercial world over time into something "better", more "worthwhile", perhaps something more "pleasing" to God. During the class that night my view changed suddenly and almost completely. I realized that I was getting ordained and staying in the secular workplace in order to make links between those two worlds. I was doing both in order to try to make clearer how the Worker, Creator God of Genesis 1 is also present in our workplace today, and how much He cares about those workplaces and cares about us in them.

Now you may accept logically what I'm saying, but do you really feel it? Many workplaces don't feel that great, don't feel like places of opportunity. There can be enormous tension.

Tyrannical bosses. Horrible colleagues. Stupid, pointless, meaningless rules. Long hours. Little sympathy or empathy. The threat of redundancy. A total lack of privacy. Or it can be even worse than that. There can be real discrimination. You might feel you are being asked to do unethical things, to cut corners. Or you may feel that the social utility of what you are doing is zero – or even negative. All of these things can make the workplace seem a bit of a nightmare. So, how on earth can God be there? Well, the simple answer is this: in the same way that He's present in the rest of our broken world. Life outside the workplace can be pretty awful sometimes, too – even in churches. Does every family get on at Christmas? Do families never viciously argue? Does every church welcome outsiders with open arms? What about clerical sexual abuse scandals? Nevertheless, despite this, do we feel that means that God cannot, therefore, be present in the midst of family, or in the midst of the church?

The point is not what's wrong; it's what could be right. And that may be unexpected – totally, completely, utterly unexpected. That is the story of Jacob's ladder. Here's Jacob. He's already tricked his stupid elder brother Esau out of his birthright, and now he impersonates him to his old, blind father Isaac, with the total support of his conniving mother Rebekah, in order to get Isaac's blessing. Esau, who's a big guy, not unreasonably is outraged when he finds out about this and, slightly less reasonably, decides to kill Jacob. Rebekah finds out and tells Jacob, and she and Isaac bundle him off out of the way to see relatives.

So, sent away, and in trouble both with his brother and also, one might hope, with his conscience, Jacob travels until it's dark and then just lies down in the countryside to go to sleep. Then the totally unexpected happens. To this dodgy character, on the run, and in the middle of nowhere – miles from the nearest shrine, and a long way from 10 a.m. on Sunday morning – God appears. And doesn't just appear, but heaven touches earth and earth touches heaven. All of a sudden everything is changed, transformed. What looked like an ordinary place is, in fact, the place where God is present, and where heaven and earth meet. In this nowhere place, God announces to Jacob that He will be with him and his successors and that they will be blessed forever.

God is not constrained by buildings, or by days of the week, or by circumstances, or by where we feel we are, or by what others think of us. God is not made in our image; it's the other way around – and, therefore, we should expect to be surprised from time to time. Jacob exclaims, "Surely the Lord is in this place – and I did not know it!... How awesome is this place! This is none other than the house of God, and this is the gate of heaven." That strikes me as a pretty good way of viewing even the worst workplace. People may think it's dodgy; they may think it's nowhere – the place that you have to go to in order to earn the money that you can then spend in order to be able to forget it – but, looked at in the right way, it may just be the gate of heaven. We must be prepared to be surprised because one thing can be almost guaranteed. If the heavens open and a ladder descends it will not – it will not – be in a church by the altar. It will almost certainly be nowhere in the building. It will surprise us – and it could very well be in your workplace.

So in these first ten chapters, we will explore where the ladder might be in your workplace, and perhaps how to find it. We'll certainly look at the bad things that can happen in any workplace, but the essential point to remember is that what we humans make bad, God can (quite often through us) make good again. So what might the opportunities be once we recognize the ladder in the workplace? Well, there are some obvious ones. It can be a place where we exercise personal responsibility and behave ethically – not fiddle our expenses, and always cut square corners (as my former boss was fond of saying). Where we can deliver an honest day's work for an honest day's pay.

But it's not just that. It can also be where we carry out the gospel imperative to care for those who are in need, for those who need help. Our fellow workers may not be literally hungry, or prisoners, or naked, as in the parable of the sheep and the goats, but there are plenty – far too many people – who in the workplace really do feel trapped. Who feel imprisoned by circumstances, imprisoned by the need to earn something, anything, to put bread on the table for their family. Imprisoned by an inability to imagine something better, or by blind ambition that drives them ever harder and, thus, also further away from friends and family. Those people are prisoners in a workplace rather than a jail.

There may be those who are starving for respect, or a little love or friendship, or just a little fulfilment – and those people are truly hungry. Or our fellow workers may feel incompetent and out of their depth, or ugly, or unbearably different. Under the spotlight in the workplace these people are in a very real sense naked. It is our job, our duty, our obligation, but also our opportunity, our privilege, to help those people in those situations wherever they may be – including in the workplace.

But it's not just that. The workplace can also be the place where we exercise our talents, our God-given talents, to reach true fulfilment. A place where we exercise our skills to create things and services that other people want and need. Where we can be the stewards that God calls us to be from the very beginning of creation. A place where, if we get it right, we can create employment that gives our fellow humans jobs that give them dignity – that allows them to look after their families. And a place where we can work imaginatively in teams giving living expression to Paul's analogy in 1 Corinthians 12 of the different parts of the body bringing their own functions and gifts to make up something which is more than the sum of its parts. That doesn't just work for the church – it can work for a secular workplace, too.

But it's not just that. It's a place where we can be co-workers in the act of healing God's creation. Where we can work for justice and for ethics. Where we can try to ensure that what our business, or government department, or school – or whatever it is – does, contributes in some way to the common good. Where, be it ever so slowly, we can try to make sure that the next decision that is taken is slightly better in some way than the previous one. A place where we can fight for what we believe – gently, respectfully, but persistently – and make a real, tangible difference to those around us, and to those whom we seek to serve.

But it's not just that. It can be a place of mission. A place where we try to bring what we know about our God, about Jesus Christ who lived and died and rose for us, to those who don't know. Now to be clear, I'm not for a moment suggesting handing out tracts or standing on a soapbox in the corridor with a megaphone. What I am suggesting, however, is that we can be who we are, that we witness to being Christians by being the people we are and by the way we act. We are much closer to many more people in the workplace than in any other area of our lives. In those close settings, day in day out, there are very few secrets. If we're Christians, they'll know it. If we act in certain ways, they'll see that. If it seems to help us in bad times and good, they'll note it. And sometimes they'll want to talk – and then we can tell them about the gift that has been given to us.

But it's not just that. There's so much more – but perhaps that's enough for now. Even when you read that partial list, however, don't you feel like Jacob? You've been looking around and everything seems pretty grim and then, all of sudden, you see the potential – heaven opens up, so to speak – and you realize, surprised, shocked, that *surely the Lord is in this place, and I did not know it*! God is there at the most unexpected times and in the most unexpected places. Heaven can touch earth when we least expect it. That is the potential of Jacob's ladder. That is the potential of the workplace. That is the potential of God at work.

2
Your Boss

Ephesians 6:1–9 (NRSV)

Children, obey your parents in the Lord, for this is right. "Honour your father and mother" – this is the first commandment with a promise: "so that it may be well with you and you may live long on the earth." And, fathers, do not provoke your children to anger, but bring them up in the discipline and instruction of the Lord. Slaves, obey your earthly masters with fear and trembling, in singleness of heart, as you obey Christ; not only while being watched, and in order to please them, but as slaves of Christ, doing the will of God from the heart. Render service with enthusiasm, as to the Lord and not to men and women, knowing that whatever good we do, we will receive the same again from the Lord, whether we are slaves or free. And, masters, do the same to them. Stop threatening them, for you know that both of you have the same Master in heaven, and with him there is no partiality.

In the first chapter, we looked at how God might be present in the workplace in the most unexpected places and the most unexpected ways. However, of all the unexpected ways in which heaven might manifest itself in the workplace, few seem less likely than something closely connected with our boss.

I remember my first boss. I was nineteen and he must have been almost three times that. He did not socialize, spoke –

literally – a different language from almost everyone else in that workplace, and was rarely seen except for the occasional explosive foray from his office to find out why someone had failed to do something. For me, as an impatient teenager, he appeared to sum up all that was tiresome, static, and unimaginative about people in their fifties drifting towards retirement. So here's the question – and even discounting heavily for the exceptional arrogance of (my) youth: what might uninspiring bosses, and tyrannical bosses, and careless bosses, and ineffective bosses have to say about where God might be in the workplace? Again, looking through the prism of the story of Jacob, is there really any chance that the heavenly ladder might actually touch down in the boss's office, and, if it did, what on earth would it mean?

To try to tease that answer out a bit, I have picked one of the most controversial passages in the Bible: "Slaves obey your earthly masters". In Richard Dawkins-land this passage sits in the front row of the accused at the Bible-Crimes Trial; Christianity in the dock as the religion of the oppressor and the bigot. How can a passage used by pre-Civil War American slave-owners to defend their holding of fellow humans as goods and chattels to be exploited, abused, and bought and sold, have anything useful to say to us about anything? Our normal reaction to this passage is either to skip it, or, if we're really forced to look at it, to come up with good reasons why it wasn't written by the "nice" Paul who wrote Romans and Corinthians. It must instead have been written later by someone else who had appropriated Paul's name in order to squeeze the church into a patriarchal, property-owning straightjacket very removed from what Jesus of Nazareth could ever have intended. But along the lines of being surprised, or never quite knowing where God will be, let's just stick with the passage for a moment longer.

Now – and I hope obviously – while we occasionally talk about being "slaves to work", or "wage slaves", I am not in any way condoning or defending, far less advocating for, slavery. However, what do we get if we replace the word "master" with "boss", and the word "slave" with "direct report" or "employee"? Well, it still rankles doesn't it? That word "obey" doesn't have a particularly twenty-first-century feel to it. What about "flat pyramids" and "cooperative workplaces" and all the other things they teach at business school? Go back to my nineteen-year-old self for a moment. Fresh out of boarding school, where "obey" had very much been the way of things, I wanted to be "free". I was determined to live the more individualistic, adult culture that I had previously watched from my schoolroom window. Deference seemed very old-fashioned – constricting, suffocating – placed against the desire and the possibilities for self-expression. Perhaps I could learn from a boss who was dynamic and charismatic, her or himself a dramatically individualistic individual. But from some grey plodder? What was there to learn?

Well, let's take a closer look at what Paul (or his evil twin) actually has to say. The key to understanding the slaves and masters passage may actually lie in the passage that immediately precedes it about parents and children. Even today we understand that kids do best when there are boundaries that they cannot cross, rules that keep them safe. Rules that allow them freedom within certain limits. Rules which perhaps allow them to protest – e.g. "I just want to be free" or "I need to express myself" – but, nevertheless, also allow them to protest in safety. Rules that allow the process of really growing up, of developing minds, of intellectual exploration, of social development, of trying things and failing – but failing in safety. That's what these boundaries for children are for: not to restrict freedom, but to allow real development. If the boundaries are drawn carefully and sympathetically, that can happen. Then, instead of spending all their time constantly trying to find out what the limits are by always pushing, by always trying to see how much farther they can go, our children can instead, within those generous boundaries, do the things and develop the skills that make them distinctive, productive, happy, fully-formed human beings.

But can this carry across to the workplace? Again, to be clear, I am not talking about bosses treating their workers as children. Remember, this is only an analogy. Many, however, will have worked in a workplace with ambitious fellow workers, or perhaps in a workplace that actively encourages rivalry as a way of increasing productivity or profit. Sometimes this is justified as being about allowing workers to be free to pursue self-expression or even self-interest – but those workplaces are often terrible places to be. It's all about self-promotion; the job is not an end in itself, or a source of pleasure or pride. It is simply a means to the next job promotion, or the next pay rise, or the next bonus. To get there you have to trample over others. To get there you have worry about how you appear, not how you are. To get there you have to worry, and worry, and worry.

So one of the things Paul is saying is that in setting boundaries, even if they seem to chafe, the boss can be doing us a favour. It can lessen the constant striving and jockeying for position and allow us to focus on the job instead of on ourselves. Paul also talks about the effect that we, as good workers, can have on a bad boss (which we'll look at in another chapter). But I want to look at another, slightly different benefit of a hierarchical management structure. In some places – Silicon Valley is always mentioned – teams with no hierarchies (the famous "flat pyramids") are held up as the business structures of tomorrow. Often, however, it seems to me, you need a decision-making structure; you need someone to make the final decision and take the responsibility. It's partly, as another of those business school sayings goes, "If everybody owns it, then nobody owns it." Someone has to be on the hook.

There can also be something more beneficial, more creative, in a business hierarchy. To look at my own work, in some cases I'm the chair, while in other cases I'm very clearly not the boss. In those different settings I behave in very different ways. As a subordinate, feeding into the process, I view my role as being to push the course I view as the best, without making the case for any other view. It is my job, there, to be in the centre of the discussion and to propose courses of action, often getting into a considerable level of detail. As chair, or boss, however, I act very differently, holding back on my arguments until others have made theirs. My role then is often strategic, rather than detailed, trying to see the big picture rather than all the details. My job, as boss, is to take the wisdom of others and synthesize it, rather than enter into the argument at the beginning and press my pre-existing point of view. A good outcome for the business as a whole requires both of those inputs (and many more, from administrative support through to effective implementation). So while I may occasionally grumble about my boss (and I am absolutely certain that many grumble about me), that structure will often produce the best results. It relates very much to the analogy that Paul uses in 1 Corinthians (and to which we will return) about a single body being made up of many parts, all of which are crucial to its proper functioning.

Before going much further we do need to look at a fundamental question: why is it important to God that the workplace functions well and that the business succeeds (beyond the basic impact on the individuals in it)? Well, the fact that we ask that question points to another of the central problems with our difficulty in finding God in the workplace that we mentioned in the first chapter – namely the relative absence of any meaningful theology of work in the church. Here we will have to go back to basics for a moment.

Martin Luther started life as a Catholic monk, but, among other things, he profoundly objected to the then current church view which placed priests and monks at the top of the work tree, with secular vocations trailing well behind. Luther's view was that God acted through everything and everyone, and therefore all work and all vocations were equally valuable. This doctrine of vocations (or "stations") is important for our general understanding of why the workplace can be somewhere where God is present. But we need to take it one step further in the case of obeying our boss to explain why a focus on our work, as opposed to on ourselves and our advancement, is important to God.

The final piece of this puzzle, therefore, relates to our place in God's creation, and our role in helping fulfil it. To go back to the creation story – or, rather, stories – in the first few chapters of Genesis, while God is the creator of the world, humanity is His partner in helping that creation reach its fulfilment. Whether you take it literally or metaphorically, the second creation story does speak a fundamental truth:

> *In the day that the Lord God made the earth and the heavens, when no plant of the field was yet in the earth and no herb of the field had yet sprung up – for the Lord God had not caused it to rain upon the earth, and there was no one to till the ground; then the Lord God formed man… [And the] Lord God took the man and put him in the Garden of Eden to till it and keep it. (Genesis 2:4–7, 15 NRSV)*

The simple point is that God's creation is ongoing, working towards that final time at which everything will be made perfect

– and we are God's hands and feet on earth to do that "tilling". As discussed above, imperfection crept into creation, so the ongoing action also relates to the healing and redemption of that creation. This requires us to work with God now. It is an incredibly empowering statement about work: work itself can be holy, and whatever distracts us from that, or distracts us from doing it well, is a detriment to creation. To be clear, that doesn't just mean tilling the fields or making something beautiful. It is about the wise use of the world's resources for the goal of human flourishing – which most definitely includes being in a workplace, whether you're providing services, facilitating manufacturing, or helping to run a government.

To go back to Paul: if we're obeying our boss, accepting the chain of command so that we can effectively work for God, that should – in the best of circumstances – be a win-win. First, we remove from ourselves the stress of always having to determine where the boundaries are. When we know where they are, we can focus instead on our work. In doing the work itself, there is also the possibility that we understand (however imperfectly) that what we are doing is in partnership with God himself, the ultimate boss – and that, too, can give us huge satisfaction.

There's so much more that needs to be unpacked on this aspect of the vocation of work. And, yes, there's a series of problems that we also need to consider. The world is not a perfect place, so, for example, what happens if your boss is a bad person, or represents a bad power structure, or your work feels morally challenging? We'll come back to some of these in the next chapter when we look at this from the other end – the perspective of the direct report. The purpose of this chapter is to show the potentiality of the position – how God might be present, how heaven might touch earth, however counterintuitive it initially seems, through the figure of our boss.

So the next time you're sitting in your boss's office cursing her restrictions, or his incompetence, or her plain nastiness, try to put that aside. Paul's real point was not to prop up the power structure of his day (or of our day) but, in fact, to set us free – free to be creative, and free to be with God. It is in God, through participation with God – including in work – that we can find that freedom. So this is not in any way about justifying or perpetuating slavery, about keeping us under a human yoke. It is about giving us space, freed from our own fears and ambitions, in a structure where we can make a difference – where we can be co-workers with God.

3

Your Direct Report[1]

Leviticus 25:39–43 (NRSV)

If any who are dependent on you become so impoverished that they sell themselves to you, you shall not make them serve as slaves. They shall remain with you as hired or bound labourers. They shall serve with you until the year of the jubilee. Then they and their children with them shall be free from your authority; they shall go back to their own family and return to their ancestral property. For they are my servants, whom I brought out of the land of Egypt; they shall not be sold as slaves are sold. You shall not rule over them with harshness, but shall fear your God.

The last chapter considered the role played by our boss in the workplace, and how some hierarchy and boundaries might free us to better serve God by being able to enjoy our work and thereby participate in the ongoing work of His creation. I hope, however, slightly unpalatable though that message about boundaries and obedience may have been, we can regard it as the necessary vegetables before

---

1   Some people have told me that the term "direct report" may not be widely understood in the UK. A direct report is someone who reports directly to you as that employee's manager (although that person may, in turn, have their own direct reports). In org chart terms, they have a "solid" line connecting them to you (as opposed to a "dotted" or indirect line that indicates a more informal relationship). While the direct report must follow the manager's instructions, there is (or should be) a mutuality to the relationship whereby the manager is responsible for providing feedback and support to the direct report, and assisting in career development.

we turn to the dessert. It is in considering how the boss can transform the workplace for those who work for him or her that the potential of the workplace can perhaps more clearly be seen. Now, I am aware (as I will say again and again) that many workplaces can be awful, that the business that operates that workplace may be in some way corrupt, that the products and services may truly not be for the good of humankind, or that the place may encourage harsh treatment of subordinates. But remember what we are looking for is not the perfect workplace – nice though that would be – but for potential, for the unexpected. So, again, the purpose of this chapter is to search for the potentiality for transformation, in relation to how a boss's treatment of his or her direct reports might suddenly reveal that connection between earth and heaven, and the meaning of what we are doing.

The Bible passage for this chapter, as with the one for the last, however, must get over one hurdle before we even start, and that is the issue of hierarchy. I will come back to this at the end, but it is clear that hierarchy in the world is accepted as a fact in both the Old and the New Testaments. In this, hierarchy is rather like money – essentially neutral until humans make it either bad or good. Jesus uses many parables which assume the presence of a hierarchy, in which, according to the lessons He wanted to teach from the story, the master is either good or bad, or the servant is either faithful or unfaithful: vineyard owners, rulers, the father of the Prodigal Son. But this hierarchy – or inequality if you prefer to see it another way – is a fact of life. Our modern individualism rebels against that, but in fact it's what we humans do with hierarchy, including in the workplace, that makes the difference – and that's what we'll explore.

The Bible passage for this chapter, this time from the Old Testament, carries echoes of the one from Paul in the previous chapter. At the end Paul wrote about how owners should not threaten their slaves. Now while it was a step forward for Paul to call for this in relation to slaves, there was a much longer-standing Old Testament tradition that called for better treatment of workers (as opposed to slaves). Leviticus and the other books of the Torah (the first five books of the Old Testament) contain rules for how the Jewish people were to live. But these books also told, interwoven with the Law of Moses, the story of the Jewish people – of how they were held in slavery in Egypt, rescued by God, and led by Moses towards the Promised Land. This folk memory of being slaves and being liberated reverberates throughout the Old Testament. Even though from time to time the people forgot about that slavery, even though they got themselves a king, even though they got themselves a nobility, got themselves a lazy, greedy, ruling class, the prophets were always there to remind them where they had come from and how they should treat all of their brothers and sisters. And in this chapter in Leviticus we read of the rule on Jubilee: the re-setting of the clock, the undoing of any advantage, the setting free of workers who had stumbled and fallen into hardship. It's a powerful message to anyone who wants to be a good boss. The application of "Jubilee" to workers is a remarkable message in terms of transforming the workplace.

How many workplaces reflect this transformative ideal? Very few, I suspect. Reality, the world, the need and/or desire for profit all get in the way. But this is something we need to strive for, and this again is where the church is missing in action. We should be in there – and not just "the church", but all Christians – equipping business leaders to realize how transformative their role can be. A priest may see tens or, if they're lucky, a few hundred people for an hour or so on a Sunday. A boss will see the same number for forty or more hours a week. What an influence for good – or bad – that could be. What a chance to make a difference in the lives of people: to help them find fulfilment in their work; to encourage them to grow; to build a community in a team, and to help one another, especially those among them in need. All of that is not just a selfless giving, because the boss, too, gets something back in terms of fulfilment and development.

Let me just talk a little about my own experience. As I mentioned in the introduction, I work for a very large American corporation and have a fairly grand-sounding title, but I actually haven't had direct reports for very long. But now I have them, and it is slowly changing my outlook. It's a responsibility, to start off with: finding work; deciding the division of labour between what you should do and what they should do; giving direction; finding the appropriate line between encouragement and constructive criticism. In some ways it's not unlike being a parent – but with the enormous difference that they are adults. It has made me think about the next generation and how they get trained. In some respects it has made me think a little more about others and a little less about myself. Am I doing it perfectly – well, I'm sure if you asked those people, they'd tell you definitely not! But am I trying? Yes. And why? Because I am a Christian. I understand the need for the company to make a profit. I'm proud of the things we make and the services we provide. And I am quite prepared to make tax policy arguments on behalf of my company that, especially in today's climate, not everyone may like. But I view all of that – including the way I treat those who report to me – through the prism of Christianity. Sure it's about responsibility, but it's also about the opportunity to transform the workplace.

So, in light of that, I want to look at four ways in which the impact of a boss may be transformative on his or her direct reports. They all interlock – a sort of matrix or, if you prefer, a chart with two axes and four quadrants. The first two of these are personal. How does the boss potentially transform the relationships in the workplace by her actions towards, and in front of, her employees? And, how does the boss influence those employees by the way he interacts with the company? Linked to these first two are more institutional effects. How does the boss affect the nature and quality of the work her direct reports undertake? And how does the boss affect the spirit and ethos of the company by his own actions?

So, let's take the first of those – the influence of the boss by the way she conducts herself. This is fairly straightforward, and there are direct and indirect effects. The direct effect relates to how the boss treats her direct reports. If she is considerate, fair, helpful, then that will make life pleasant for the direct reports. If she is none of those, then life will be much less pleasant – and that will affect, at some level, how much they put into their work. There is also the indirect effect. If she is honest, there's a good chance her direct reports will be – and if she's dishonest, they may be much more likely also to be dishonest. Pleasant or nasty, respectful or bullying, she will set the example that will often be followed. It comes down to what we read in Paul in the previous chapter, and Leviticus in this chapter. Treat well those over whom you have power, and encourage them to do good.

The second effect – how the boss reacts to the company – is a little more complicated. One aspect may be how your boss treats his boss. If he – to use a colloquialism – "kisses up and kicks down" then that's a terrible example to set. It sends incredibly negative signals about hierarchy, about raw power, and about how to behave to those more and less powerful than you. Another, equally important aspect of this is how he does (or does not) demonstrate integrity. How does he react to things that are wrong, or that go wrong? Does he cover up, or try to change things? Is he open with his employees, and does he discuss these issues with them? Again, obvious points, but these make a huge difference not just to the atmosphere in the workplace, but to the quality of what his direct reports do there. In short, for good or bad, it affects their characters – and that's quite a responsibility.

In addition to these first two effects, however, which are personal in that they come down to character and the impact of example on other humans, there are also more institutional effects. So for instance, how does the boss encourage her direct reports in their work? How does she develop them, allow them to learn, to reach their full potential? Hang on a moment, you're thinking, isn't that just about profit maximization through more efficient workers? Well, certainly that might be one of the outcomes, but also think about what we've said about human participation in helping to heal and redeem the potential of creation. In the previous chapter we looked at Martin Luther's doctrine of vocations, but there is a modern update on this which deals with some of the issues raised by modernity and the move away from small-town life where everything was ordered and people knew their role, to large, impersonalized, mechanized cities. Miroslav Volf, a Croatian theologian (now in the US), talks not in terms of a "station" in life in which we find ourselves, but rather about a spirit-led contribution of a charism or gift by each person. It's hard to explain in a sentence or two, but basically, through the contribution of our gift, making as much of it as we can, we contribute to God's creation which will be made perfect at the end of time. So what the boss can do by encouraging our development, by encouraging training, by encouraging us to reach our full potential is not just to make more money for the business (or ourselves) but also to develop and sharpen those gifts that can then be used for God. Again, this may sound a little strange – but remember we're talking about the unexpected, about something right under our noses that appears to be one thing (training) but is in fact something completely different (increasing our potential to participate in creation). And the boss helping her direct reports to lead more fulfilling lives in accordance with their gifts contributes to that.

Finally, we should look at the potentially transformative effect that the boss might have on the business for the benefit of his direct reports. We have talked about bad workplaces where the culture is oppressive, or where the business seems not to contribute to the common good. It may be difficult for one person to change that – especially if they are a middle manager, rather than the CEO – but not all change has to be dramatic or take place overnight. Change can be slow, incremental, but still good, as long as it is in the right direction. A boss who tries to do this will not only inspire his workers by that example, will not only make the workplace a place where workers are more likely to find true fulfilment in their jobs, but may also be able to make the business into a more positive contributor to the society of which it is a part – more concerned, more connected. A business, yes, which still exists to turn a profit, but a business which also recognizes that it is a member of the larger community, a part of the society which surrounds it.

I'll raise here another idea (that I mentioned in the introduction, and that I'll return to in another chapter), which I find a useful way of conducting myself inside my business. It's an idea that comes from an American Franciscan priest, Richard Rohr, who talks about living on the "edge of the inside". It's not about taking dramatic, prophetic, career-limiting stands in the workplace. It's about being loyal but also about asking questions when necessary. It's about being on the inside but close enough to the edge of that inside to keep a sense of perspective. It's not about you always being right but, rather, about realizing that sometimes the business can be wrong. A boss who tries to live by that, by always questioning – respectfully, calmly, persistently – what is going on in the office, or business, or workplace, may also be able to help transform that space. A boss who tries to live like that, may – by changing things for the better – offer his direct reports that glimpse of potential, of heaven, of the ladder coming down.

Let me finish by returning to the point about hierarchy. As with the previous chapter, hierarchy is not an end in itself; it is not something without which humanity could not be humanity. It is simply the way of the world until everything is perfected by God. So it is with Jesus, the ultimate human boss, and His direct reports, the disciples. The hierarchy is clear: teacher and taught; leader and led; God and human. But in John's Gospel there is that remarkable passage when Jesus is talking to his disciples after the Last Supper on the night before He died. First He gives them the new commandment – that they love one another – and then He goes on to say this: "You are my friends if you do what I command you. I do not call you servants any longer, because the servant does not know what the master is doing; but I have called you friends, because I have made known to you everything that I have heard from my Father" (John 15:14–15 NRSV). This won't occur in every workplace, and may not occur until the end of time, but once again, as with the idea of Jubilee in the passage from Leviticus, there is the promise that in the end all the hierarchy and the order will come to an end, and we will all be set free together. As a direct report, you may not want your boss to be a friend, and sometimes they can't be. But also remember: that is the ultimate end that God has in mind and to which we can work – even in the workplace.

4
The Team

1 Corinthians 12:4–27 (NRSV)

Now there are varieties of gifts, but the same Spirit; and there are varieties of services, but the same Lord; and there are varieties of activities, but it is the same God who activates all of them in everyone. To each is given the manifestation of the Spirit for the common good. To one is given through the Spirit the utterance of wisdom, and to another the utterance of knowledge according to the same Spirit, to another faith by the same Spirit, to another gifts of healing by the one Spirit, to another the working of miracles, to another prophecy, to another the discernment of spirits, to another various kinds of tongues, to another the interpretation of tongues. All these are activated by one and the same Spirit, who allots to each one individually just as the Spirit chooses. For just as the body is one and has many members, and all the members of the body, though many, are one body, so it is with Christ. For in the one Spirit we were all baptised into one body – Jews or Greeks, slaves or free – and we were all made to drink of one Spirit. Indeed, the body does not consist of one member but of many. If the foot would say, "Because I am not a hand, I do not belong to the body," that would not make it any less a part of the body. And if the ear would say, "Because I am not an eye, I do not belong to the body," that would not make it any less a part of the body. If the whole body were an eye, where would the hearing be? If the whole body were hearing, where would the sense of smell be? But as it is, God arranged the members in the body, each one of them, as he chose. If all were a single member, where would the body be? As it is, there are many members, yet one body. The eye cannot say to the hand, "I have no need of you," nor again the head to the feet, "I have no need of you." On the contrary, the members of the body that seem to be weaker are indispensable, and those members of the body that we think less honourable we clothe with greater honour, and our less respectable members are treated with greater respect; whereas our more respectable members do not need this. But God has so arranged the body, giving the greater honour to the inferior member, that there may be no dissension within the body, but the members may have the same care for one another. If one member suffers, all suffer together with it; if one member is honoured, all rejoice together with it. Now you are the body of Christ and individually members of it.

One of the most overworked of all the oft-repeated management sayings is "There's no 'I' in team." In other words, rampant individualism and naked self-interest have no place in a team. Teams and teamwork are an obligatory part of any corporate speech, annual report, or management training manual. A quick Google search on the importance of teamwork in the workplace comes up with over 17 million results. Yet the evidence in front of our eyes tells us that it rarely happens quite like that.

I once worked for a US law firm that prided itself on its "collegiality" between partners, but practised, at least from what I could see, nothing of the sort. If a partner brought in business then that partner jealously guarded it, rarely involved fellow partners (instead using a team of junior lawyers), and claimed that any work subsequently flowing from that client belonged just to him or her. The result was that some "partners" were just as much employees as the rest of us. Partnership relations were rancorous, and meetings were dominated by the heavy hitters who would threaten to walk if they didn't get their own way. The social niceties were just about observed, but the atmosphere was poisonous. Why? Money. The compensation system rewarded those who brought in business and penalized those who didn't. It's not uncommon, but it's completely divisive. People who should pull together, who should pool skills, instead are either constantly looking over their shoulder or are looking enviously upwards at those who treat them, at best, as poor relations. (And, of course, that affected all of us who worked there – the whole team – not just the partners.) The firms have a name for this type of compensation system that sums it all up: "Eat what you kill." So there may be no "I" in team, but it turns out that if you scramble "team" up, it can instead become "meat"...

But, again, our purpose in these first ten chapters, while acknowledging how imperfect (to put it mildly) many workplaces are, is to look for the potentiality. And when it comes to teamwork the potentiality is very real, because "team" and "teamwork" are not just corporate slogans but genuinely transformative ideas.

In this Bible passage Paul is writing to the constantly troubled, argumentative, and divided church in Corinth. He points out to them one essential thing, which he then illustrates in a couple of ways. You are, he tells them, one body – the body of Christ – and you are all equipped for participation in that body by gifts from the Holy Spirit. At the same time, however, all of those gifts are different, yet in some way – even if not always immediately obviously – they are complementary to each other. So something may appear to be an unimportant gift, but, just like a seemingly unimportant part of the body, in fact those gifts are essential to the functioning of the whole. So, for example, workplaces need cleaners and photocopy repair folks, as well as the boss and the ideas guy. Together they make up the body, the unit, the team that allows the business to function. Paul says to be respectful of every job, because each charism comes from God, and each is precious to Him. So here we have a model for the team. Everyone brings something to the table; everyone should be valued. But the point is also made from the other end – in the same way that the body cannot function efficiently without one of its parts, neither can one of those parts make up the whole body on its own. We need the team to reach our own highest potential, in the same way that the team needs us to reach its. To boil this down into another well-known management teamwork saying: "None of us is as smart as all of us."

But is Paul preaching impossible perfection? Well, let's return to a team we touched on briefly in the last chapter: Jesus' disciples, the Twelve. Even putting aside the HR disaster of hiring Judas Iscariot, they don't always look like a single, well-oiled machine. Just to pick a few random examples: they go to pieces in a boat when they're out on a sales trip and a storm picks up. They're hopeless at selling this healing product – even when the boss shows them how to do it. They constantly fail to understand the explanations of how to demonstrate the product. They constantly forget the corporate mission statement that He's telling them. And there's more than a streak of vanity in one or two of them. Rather than all pulling together, they argue about who is the greatest among them; and in one case Mummy is sent in to ask the boss if her two boys can sit on either side of Him at what they seem to think will be the annual office party. Finally, when the boss appears to get taken out, they go to pieces, and the designated successor – Peter – denies several times that he's even a member of the team. That's not going to get used as the Harvard Business School case study of sales team success.

But then something happens – the boss somehow inspires

them – and they do come together as a team. Suddenly they can speak the client's language – actually the language of all the clients. They find they have a convincing sales pitch. They can now deliver the goods – healing – and immediately they start taking market share. In a completely unexpected move, one of their chief rivals decides to join them and they start expanding into foreign markets. And the result: 2,000 years later the brand is still going, with, currently, over 2 billion more or less satisfied customers. That is the team that God: Father, Son, and Holy Spirit built. And the model works.

Now what happened to the disciples in the upper room at Pentecost – the coming of the Holy Spirit with tongues of fire – may seem unlikely to translate itself over to your conference room at a Monday morning staff meeting, or to a get-together in the staff cafeteria. But, again, be prepared to be surprised.

In the last chapter we looked a little at Miroslav Volf. His idea is that the workplace is where – by exercising our charisms or gifts – we can best help God by contributing to the healing and fulfilment of His creation. That's also what Paul is talking about in his letter to the church at Corinth – using the gifts we have been given to make the whole more than the sum of the parts. Or, to flip around that saying I used earlier: *to show that all of us are smarter than any one of us.* So to marry those two thoughts together – the exercising of our gifts, and the ability of a good team to be better than the sum of its parts – we are most likely to be able to discover and then use those gifts effectively in God's service inside a functioning team. In the midst of a proper, functioning team, therefore, may be precisely the place that Jacob's ladder touches down in the workplace.

Of course, it may not be obvious at first. As we considered in the previous chapter, a boss getting better training for her employees may look like a totally profit-inspired move. But if it also enables her workers to function better as a team and to recognize their potential, then it also has a godly purpose (the two can coexist). Building a better team is important for each team member and is important for God.

But there's more to it than that. There's also the mutual support and encouragement of a well-functioning team in the workplace that makes life better. If we show respect for the gifts of others, then we help to grow their self-respect. It is also demonstrably true that people will work better when confident than unconfident. Those outcomes, it turns out – while, yes, perhaps also increasing productivity and profit – will make those people happier and fulfilled; will make them closer to the ideal of beings created in their Maker's image. This mutual support is powerful, and is summed up by another of those business sayings: "Teamwork enables ordinary people to do extraordinary things." It really does.

There's still more to it than that. Most people have problems – emotional, financial, or familial – whether they're the boss, or the cleaner, or the sales rep, or the middle manager. And in most workplaces they spend a lot of time together. That can be an opportunity. An opportunity for that team – that community – to help with healing. An opportunity to engage in feeding the metaphorically hungry, clothing the metaphorically naked, visiting the metaphorically imprisoned that we looked at in the first chapter. God acts through people, and not just in the slum or barrio, but in the workplace, in the next cubicle along. All of creation needs healing; all of creation is important to God. God gives us that opportunity to participate by proximity to those in need. God may act through priests, he may act through Sunday school teachers, through nurses, through doctors. But He may also act through bosses and co-workers, even the apparently least important members of the team. Again, we should be prepared to be surprised.

There's still more to it than that. As Christians we are

called upon to love our neighbours, and often we have difficulty figuring out what that means. We are expected to love our families and our friends. In the workplace what the term "neighbour" actually means – someone not otherwise connected to us by bonds of blood or affection – becomes clear. It's our team: it's the woman in the office next to ours; it's the man in the cubicle next to ours. That is our neighbour, our fellow team member, and we have the opportunity of being able to help them. We don't have to seek them out. They are right there under our noses. We don't have to be trained therapists or anything like that in order to help. We just have to listen, we just have to care, and we just have to be our unobtrusive Christian selves. To be clear, this is not about overt evangelizing, and our neighbour can be Christian, or Jewish, or Muslim, or Hindu, or atheist. They are all our neighbours – as much as the Israelite was to the Samaritan. Being part of a team gives us the opportunity to love our neighbour, to help our neighbour. Might that also help the productivity of the team on the bottom line? Sure. But God can work like that.

Of course, not every team works like this. I started this chapter talking about an entire firm that adopted the language of the team but did not really live it. What if there's a member of the team who messes it all up despite everyone else's best efforts – someone who doesn't pull his weight, or who always seems to sour the atmosphere? What if there's someone so selfish, so individualistic, that she seems to ruin it for everyone else, by never sharing opportunities that the team could use better? Well we'll look at that when we come to the annoying colleague in a later chapter, but I firmly believe that the team can truly be a godly thing.

As I opened with a personal story, let me also finish with one. After that early experience, I have now spent many years working with a remarkable group of people, and, with only one or two exceptions, we really do function as a team. We complement each other's strengths and make up for each other's weaknesses. We are, across the board, the complete range from chalk to cheese; that full range of different gifts (and characters) that Paul talks about in our passage from Corinthians – and the whole really does add up to more than the sum of the parts. But, additionally, within that group there is also both caring and the opportunity to help others. The support that we receive when things have gone wrong at home, when relationships have broken up, when spouses have died, when serious illness has come, has all been remarkable.

But the support that I/we can give to others is equally important – the team creates enough trust for someone to accept my help. It's not a sign of weakness, not a sign of failure that will be taken into account at the next salary review; it's the act of a loving neighbour, and it's received as such. But supporting others may not always be as obvious as comforting the bereaved. I've slowly found, however, that being a priest in the workplace who's not afraid to say that he lives in a grey zone, not afraid to say that he worries about the ambiguities of what he does, not afraid to say that he sometimes feels uncomfortable with what he has to do, actually is also a support to others – to the team – who have the same feelings and concerns but thought they were alone and had to keep quiet. This sharing of doubts – in some ways the sharing of vulnerability – is also something that can be done within a true team. Put slightly differently, within a functioning team we can have the strength to acknowledge our weaknesses, and thereby gain the freedom from our fears in order to be more truly human.

Your team may not be perfect (in fact it almost certainly isn't), but it still offers the chance – offers each of us, together and individually, the chance – to work with God. We must be prepared to be surprised in the workplace – because it may, in fact, be whole teams of angels going up and down Jacob's ladder.

5

The Office Gossip

James 3:6–10 (NRSV)

And the tongue is a fire. The tongue is placed among our members as a world of iniquity; it stains the whole body, sets on fire the cycle of nature, and is itself set on fire by hell. For every species of beast and bird, of reptile and sea creature, can be tamed and has been tamed by the human species, but no one can tame the tongue – a restless evil, full of deadly poison. With it we bless the Lord and Father, and with it we curse those who are made in the likeness of God. From the same mouth come blessing and cursing. My brothers and sisters, this ought not to be so.

What harm can a bit of gossip be? It's really only a little innocent fun. It's not like you're hurting someone by doing it to their face. And, besides which, it's probably all true. The person you're telling it to is sworn to confidence, so it won't go anywhere. And, anyway, when it really comes right down to it, the person sort of deserves it.

These, as you'll recognize – especially if you've made them yourselves – are all pretty feeble rationalizations. Gossip is, in fact, almost always debasing for at least three different people: for the person gossiped about; for the gossiper; and, slightly less obviously, for the person listening to the gossip. Just to illustrate that last point, I still recall a piece of office gossip from many years ago that I profoundly wish I'd never heard. A friend from work told me that she had been talking to a fellow worker, and this other person had indicated how easy it had been to get yet another work friend into bed. This other friend was married, happily I had thought. I had known her for several years, and now this – true or untrue – had got thrown into the mix of our friendship. Uninvited, uncalled for, no business of mine, yet a fact or image lodged in my head that I could never shake out. The first friend – the gossiper – topped it all off by saying that she felt she had to tell me, because I would want to know as a friend of that other person. Well, no, actually. Precisely the opposite. But once put there, once the words had been uttered, they couldn't be taken back. Something had been altered, broken, and the shape of two friendships changed for the worse. The result is real annoyance with the first friend, and awkwardness with the second, which lasts to this day. That's gossip for you.

One of the most fatuous of all the childhood sayings is the one about sticks and stones breaking our bones but words never being able to hurt us. Other than those rare humans with hides like a rhinoceros', words are capable of hurting much more than any physical injury, and that hurt is also likely to last much longer. Our bodies mend fairly easily, our souls often less so. Words are the means by which we communicate, through which we express our thoughts and our emotions. It is in words that we try to formulate our character itself – and that makes words things of immense power. Saying "they were just words" misses the point. And gossip is among the worst inflictors of pain through words. Some gossip may be true, much may be untrue, but what links the two together is the malicious intent, or grotesque carelessness, of the gossiper. Of course, they may not think of it in that way – recall the "I-thought-you-ought-to-know" reason – but in reality it will most often be about building themselves up by doing others down. Whether it's about positioning for the next promotion or bonus round, or trying to break into an influential clique by gaining popularity at someone else's expense, it damages not just the individuals involved but also the team as a whole. And diminishing the cohesion and effectiveness of the team diminishes all the members of the team.

The Bible recognizes the destructive nature of gossip very clearly both in the Old and New Testaments. "Gossip" and its synonyms are terms which frequently recur. The Hebrew term used in the Old Testament apparently means someone who reveals secrets, tells tales or is a scandal-monger. The Law of Moses contains prohibitions on it, and the Wisdom literature in the Bible, especially in the book of Proverbs, has much to say on the subject. For example: "A dishonest man spreads strife, and a whisperer separates close friends" (Proverbs 16:28 ESV). Or this: "Whoever covers an offense seeks love, but he who repeats a matter separates close friends" (Proverbs 17:9 ESV). Or this: "For lack of wood the fire goes out, and where there is no whisperer, quarrelling ceases. As charcoal to hot embers and wood to fire, so is a quarrelsome person for kindling strife. The words of a whisperer are like delicious morsels; they go down into the inner parts of the body" (Proverbs 26:20–22 ESV). And there is plenty in the New Testament. Paul attacks gossip as divisive and demeaning in a number of his letters, but some of the most forthright language can be found in the epistle of James that begins this chapter: "A restless evil, full of deadly poison." And then, echoing Jesus, who taught that it is not what goes into people's mouths in the form of food that defiles us, but what comes out in the form of words, the epistle writer declares that the mouth is a thing of iniquity placed among the other body parts.

We can see the truth of that if we transpose this over to the workplace. If the direct reports gossip about their boss, the potential of the workplace is diminished; if the boss gossips to others about his direct reports, the potential of the workplace is diminished; if team members gossip about other team members, the potential of the workplace is diminished. Gossip can cause everything to come unstuck: trust breaks down, people fail to reach their potential, and our participation in God's creation, in that healing that we have been talking about, diminishes.

So, to reiterate, gossip can affect three sets of people: the gossiper, the target, and the listener. Let's look at those a little more. The effect on the target, the person gossiped about, can range from mild annoyance at someone who is known to spread untrue rumours about everyone, to deep hurt over allegations – true or false – made with the aim of ruining careers or relationships. The effect on the listener can range from stimulating an unhealthy interest bordering on participation, to a profound sense of sadness at illusions shattered, relationships altered, leaving a feeling of having been somehow soiled. But it is for the gossiper that things are most serious. Gossip is a drug that wears off increasingly quickly. More and more is needed. The stories get crueller and more pointed, or less and less believable. People will always listen, but often with increasing loathing of the teller. Gossip in the workplace – or anywhere else – stinks. It really does.

But hang on a moment, you're thinking. Isn't he always trying to look for the potentiality for godliness in the workplace? For that place where Jacob's ladder may come down from heaven to earth? Surely not through the gossip? Well, it will clearly require some work in this case to discover that potentiality, but let's try.

The first way to try to turn things around is in the simple matter of how we react to gossip that we are told. We can argue with it – the truth of the matter. But actually, that's a little beside the point. We don't have to be puritanically disapproving; however, if we make it clear that we just don't want to gossip, make it clear that at some level it's not good for us, or for the person being talked about, or for the gossiper, then we cut off the oxygen flow. As it says above, the tongue is a fire, but if we metaphorically cut off the oxygen for that fire then it can't burn. And doing that also can be part of that unobtrusive witnessing in the workplace that we've talked about. It's not anything dramatic, but just by refusing to participate in an activity which can turn into real cruelty, we say – or rather show – something about our value system.

Secondly, of course, something godly may occur when we help the person being gossiped about. Again, we can argue against the gossip. We can tell our manager that we don't think it's true; we can tell our fellow workers that. But, again, that may be a little beside the point. The person being gossiped about will be hurting, and, as our neighbour, it is our obligation to love them, to help them. Think about the parable of the Good Samaritan. There's nothing in that story on the character of the injured man. He didn't have to be a good human being for the Samaritan to help him. He just had to be in need. Jesus understood the power – the hurtful power – of gossip. The Pharisees, after all, gossiped about Him the whole time. Did you see whom He had dinner with last night? A sinner! Did you see whose house He went to yesterday? A dirty tax collector's! Did you see what that woman did with her hair and blubbering all over His feet? She's a tart! Yes, Jesus understood about gossip. So, again, our task, our way of witnessing to the love of God, is to love the person gossiped about regardless of whether the gossip is true or false. If it's true and bad, then other procedures exist for sorting that out – but we're still obliged to love that person. However, if it's trivial, or malicious, or untrue, then that person will be hurting badly – and possibly for a long time. To return to another parable we've looked at before, the sheep and the goats, don't for a moment imagine that gossip won't leave someone metaphorically naked, or starving, or imprisoned. Gossip, the web of words, the pushing of someone out of the circle, will achieve all of those things far more effectively than anything physical. But by reaching out to that person we can help them as a Christian, as a human being.

Finally, the godly potential may be present in helping the gossiper. I don't want to talk about this too much because of the possible overlap with the topic of "the annoying colleague" in a later chapter, but we should be aware that gossipers themselves may well be in need of help. Gossip is often a sign of weakness, not strength. The person doing the gossiping is often trying to bring others – both those they're talking about and those they're talking to – down to their level: the murky, miserable place where they find themselves to be. That's not to condone the gossiper, but if we can find a way to help them then two benefits may follow: that person is helped, and, just as importantly, the workplace, the community, whatever the larger group is, is helped because the gossip is closed down at its source. The tap is turned off.

Now, again, I'm aware that even in talking about the godly potential the tone has remained slightly negative. There can be godliness in counteracting the gossip in various ways – including the opportunity to help others. Overall, however, the message is that gossip is bad. But is there another way of looking at this? Obviously the opposite of "gossiping" is "not gossiping", but is there any way that it might also be "positive gossiping"? Is silence the only alternative to gossip? Is what all of this adds up to contained in another of those sayings: "If you can't find something good to say about someone then don't say anything"? No, I really do think we can find more than that.

In his letter to the Ephesians, Paul tells the community there, "Let no evil talk come out of your mouths, but only what is useful for building up, as there is need, so that your words may give grace to those who hear" (Ephesians 4:29 NRSV). In other words, don't gossip – not just "don't gossip", but also "say positive things". Say things that will build people up, that will build up the community.

We always complain that there's only ever bad news on the television, in the same way that we only ever hear negative gossip. But the reasons for both are exactly the same: the gossiper and the listener, the supply and the demand. On the supply side, perhaps we can set an example by only telling good stories about people in the workplace. Of course, we have to be very careful not to come off as judgmental of negative gossips, or as sounding unbelievably twee and Pollyanna-ish in proposing a Boy Scout pact to only tell nice stories. But I believe we can find positive things to say about almost anyone. And it's not rocket science that people like, and respond to, sincere praise. It might just work.

The other aspect of this is the demand side: the effect that we as the listener or consumer of gossip can have on the product. If we make it clear that we will not listen to negative gossip, but that we do like to hear positive things, then maybe that demand will reshape the supply. Maybe people will be encouraged to pass on good news about other people. Again, I am aware that this sounds rather twee. It must be done non-judgmentally, and must avoid the usual "Christian" traps of being seen to criticize things that most other people find enjoyable (the list is almost endless). But even a little good news will make the workplace a much happier place – as Paul says, the words will be "useful for building up" the individuals and the community.

I want to finish by touching again on the power of words

and why we must pay attention to the ones we use. They can be a great gift. They can allow us to help other people; they can allow us to express the highest of emotions – love itself; and they can allow us to proclaim the good news that Jesus Christ died to save us. But they can also be used as weapons – violent, vicious, eviscerating weapons that wound and cripple other people. Even if not consciously used as weapons, they can still hurt deeply, profoundly, if they are used carelessly, or selfishly, or misguidedly. That is particularly true of gossip. We can't undo those words once they have been said. The tongue really does have a potential to be a fire, to torch relationships, to burn the community. If in the workplace we can prevent words from catching fire, and, even better, if we can use words positively to build people up, then we will have done something rather unusual – something rather godly.

6
Open Plan

Matthew 14:13–20 (NRSV)

Now when Jesus heard this, he withdrew from there in a boat to a deserted place by himself. But when the crowds heard it, they followed him on foot from the towns. When he went ashore, he saw a great crowd; and he had compassion for them and cured their sick. When it was evening, the disciples came to him and said, "This is a deserted place, and the hour is now late; send the crowds away so that they may go into the villages and buy food for themselves." Jesus said to them, "They need not go away; you give them something to eat." They replied, "We have nothing here but five loaves and two fish." And he said, "Bring them here to me." Then he ordered the crowds to sit down on the grass. Taking the five loaves and the two fish, he looked up to heaven, and blessed and broke the loaves, and gave them to the disciples, and the disciples gave them to the crowds. And all ate and were filled.

Put it down to my personality, or put it down to my schooldays. It doesn't really matter which. Either way the result is that I am not a huge fan of open plan workplaces. At school there were dormitories shared with eleven other boys; studies shared with three or four; classrooms with twenty or thirty; libraries with a hundred. Personal, private space was hard to come by, and the rest of my life seems to have been a reaction against that. So, it was something of a shock a few years ago when, as my business was rationalizing its work space, it became clear that the only way I could stay in central London was by moving to an open plan office. My colleagues were a great group of people – really nice – but there were a couple of immediate and pretty obvious issues. They were mostly in their mid-twenties; I was double that. One of their main jobs was to sell stuff, occasionally loudly, over the phone; mine was to try to think through a long-term strategy for our tax policy and, occasionally, to speak, much more quietly, on the phone to people who were definitely not in open plan offices. Their jobs involved planning events and going out with clients in the evening, and then discussing all about it the next morning; my only interest at the end of the day was going home to collapse. Put simply, and not in any way elevating my work over theirs (because they really did a fabulous job), mine involved thinking and theirs involved action. It was not, from my point of view at least, the perfect mix.

Most of us suspect that it is the bean counters – the people trying to shave every penny off corporate expense, regardless of the effect on real human beings – who have driven so many of us into open plan. In fact, there was actually some well-intentioned theory behind its introduction. The idea started in Germany after the Second World War but was popularized and commercialized by an American, Robert Propst, in the 1960s. Of course, there had always been large open spaces where people worked together – starting in the eighteenth and nineteenth centuries there were factories, counting houses and, more recently, secretarial pools – but these had been for relatively repetitive, almost interchangeable jobs. What changed in the 1960s was that other jobs, both those that involved talking, such as sales, and those that involved thinking and creating, such as design teams, moved into open plan. The original impetus was an insight that separate offices with walls and doors divided people, impeded the creative flow, and gave too easy an expression to hierarchy. Square footage, windows, and corner locations sent very clear messages about who mattered more and who mattered less. The natural flow of a design project, or work stream, or other project was disrupted because instead of the right teams sitting together, and the next stage of the process flowing naturally from the one before, everyone was in their own little space, often along linear corridors, communicating less efficiently and less dynamically. And so to release energy, to make for what Propst – in an admittedly rather 1960s phrase – called a more "kinetic, active, alert, and vigorous environment", companies began to move to open plan. But, of course, not quite in the way Propst had envisaged. Instead of his liberating vision, most of us got Dilbert's[2] cubicle.

That was the vision, and, if we're trying to be positive, to find that unexpected place where God might be in the workplace, there is definitely potential in open plan. There is no doubt that being in a traditional office, with four walls and a door, cuts us off from other human beings. We may spend our time working intensively, or looking out of the window, or surfing the internet, but whatever else we're doing we're not mixing with other people. We may go out to the coffee room, or canteen, or library, or meeting room, but our default position, the thing that shapes our expectations in the workplace, is to be, and to work, alone. Well, that sounds pretty good, many of you will say. But remember what we've said previously about teamwork and also about our ability to help others in the workplace who are hurting. Those both come about much less easily if we each sit in our own little cocoon, creating our own

---

2   Dilbert is a US cartoon strip by Scott Adams, with a decidedly dark view of office life. See www.dilbert.com

individual reality. In relation to teamwork, we become more a group of individuals, and less of a team, the more time we spend separated by walls. And the less we are a team, the less opportunity we have for creative interaction that Paul talked about in 1 Corinthians, with each element of the body making up a whole that is greater than the sum of the parts. It is in that environment of the team that we more easily reach our true potential, and in which we contribute our work to God and His creation. Likewise, in relation to helping others, if we live our own individual lives in our own little worlds we will be much less attuned to the needs, to the pain, of others in the workplace – our neighbours. To be sure, if we are to help them not all of that can be worked out in public. But to be in a position to discern whether something is wrong in the first place, we need to be somewhere where we have enough contact to be able to recognize it.

Now I'm not going to pretend that everything about open plan is perfect, not least because it is an experience that I don't myself particularly enjoy (or always find productive). But the reason for that is, at least in part, what we humans have done to it. Robert Propst worked for an American company that made modular furniture – i.e. sections that could be fitted together. Unfortunately, most purchasers took the smallest pieces that allowed them to fit the most people into the smallest space. Additionally, they used other features – chest-high partitions, waist-high partitions, or no partitions at all – to continue to indicate status. And since then things have often got even worse. It may make sense to have a sales team or engineering design team in open plan so that they can swap ideas and experiences. It makes less sense (although, of course, this is classic special pleading by me) to have, for example, lawyers with individual clients or a need to study and concentrate, in open plan where the distractions are all too frequent.

The problem is with a one-size-fits-all rule. Some of us are introverts who need silence to recharge our batteries. Others are extroverts who draw positive energy from a crowd. Some jobs require serious thinking time. Others require a spur to action that comes from seeing everyone else pulling for the team at the same time. There's a balance to be struck, and that balance will differ depending on the business. But the point to which I want to return is that the more healthy default position is that we start off working together and then seek privacy in offices as and when needed – rather than starting off in offices and then occasionally emerging to mingle.

If we look at the life of Jesus, for example, He spent a lot of time alone, in prayer and contemplation. Most notable is His forty days in the wilderness, as well as many other occasions when we are told that He withdrew to a mountainside or some other quiet place. But all of His major work was done in crowds. In the reading from Matthew, we hear of the feeding of the 5,000. Jesus had gone to be alone, but the crowd followed Him and He responded to them. He fed them. And there are so many similar stories: the feeding of the 4,000, all of His teaching, all of His healing – almost none of these was done with just one or even a handful of people. When the woman with bleeding touched the hem of His robe and was cured, for example, we are told He was in the midst of a crowd. So the default work position for Jesus was to be in the midst of people, with some private time to recharge the batteries. He worked in open plan, not in an office.

And so it also was for the early disciples. They worked together in crowds. From the day of Pentecost onwards they were with the people. Paul sought out crowds wherever he went, whether in the synagogues, or where the women went to wash their clothes, or in the Areopagus in Athens. Their work was with people, not on their own. Prayer was important.

Time alone with God was critical. But their work, their job, was in the midst of people, instructing them, helping them, healing them. So their default position, and ours, should be that we will be more fulfilled and more able to do God's work if we start off in the midst of people, even if we have to withdraw from the crowd from time to time.

Having extolled the possibilities of open plan, and its potential as a platform for our Christian obligation to be in the midst of others, there is one recent open plan development that doesn't help: so-called hot-desking. No longer do you have an assigned place in the open plan, a spot where you can put up photos, desk mementoes, and other things that personalize your space and connect you to it. Instead you may get assigned a locker to keep your personal stuff in, and then you sit wherever there's a space. To me this kills stone dead the godly potential of open plan. There is no teamwork potential because you have as little contact with others as you would if everyone were in individual offices. You have no chance of observing people long enough to see whether they are hurting and then being able to help. And you, yourself, feel rootless and unvalued. All of this tells people that they are essentially transient, interchangeable employees – rather like the anonymous, modular furniture at which they temporarily sit. People are not encouraged to think of themselves as being in any relationship with the company (or other employees) other than as a supplier of eight hours of individual labour each day. The short-term cost-savings might make sense (although I think, in fact, productivity is impacted almost immediately), but long term it is complete foolishness.

So, to return to our main theme, how best might we encourage the godly potentiality of open plan? Twenty years ago some of the major high-tech companies in Silicon Valley realized that their engineers and designers were not at their most productive in large open plan offices, and neither were they in individual offices opening out onto a long corridor. So they set about designing offices that looked out onto common spaces with sight lines so that people could see their fellow workers, but which at the same time gave them the privacy when they needed it to avoid time-wasting disturbances. And it can be done in other ways. One of the partners at one of the Big Four accounting firms recently gave me a tour of their new offices in London. For all but those senior staff with confidentiality requirements, the professional staff sit in open plan. But there are then countless areas where teams small and large can meet in either formal or informal settings. There are also places where individuals can go and sit either to work or relax in peace for a while. It employs the same insights. You have the team, the space to be with them, but also the space to be alone. Of course, it doesn't always – perhaps often – work like that. But when we stay connected to the team, in among the crowd, then there is the possibility for something more than just work to occur. The possibility for the ladder to touch down and for something godly to happen.

Let me finish with another story about the open plan space where I ended up being for about a year. And this shows yet another aspect of the godly potential for open plan – that of quiet, unobtrusive witnessing, or, if that's a word that sounds a little off-putting, then perhaps "influencing by example". As I've mentioned before, everyone at work knows that I'm a priest, but I don't exactly shout it from the rooftops. I have a small, unobtrusive cross on my desk and a photo of my ordination, but that's it. A few Easters ago, on Maundy Thursday, I had three services spread through the day, but I also had to be at work in between. What I normally do – a sort of cut-rate Superman – is to pop into the toilet in the clergy office at church and swap my shirt and tie for a clerical shirt and collar. But that day was just too busy, so I went into work wearing a clerical shirt without the white collar insert. Most of the sales team were there, including my favourite, the leader, who was a fifty-something Welsh atheist. "Oh, look at that," he said, "aren't you trendy today, all in black!" Then he looked a little closer and his face creased into an enormous grin as he saw the space where the white collar would normally be. "Stupid me!" he said. But for the rest of that day, he and all the others had smiles whenever they saw me – perhaps because it was Easter, perhaps because we were coming up to a four-day weekend. Who really knows? But I thought then, and think now, that they felt in some way, at some level, a little better about where they were. Because a Christian was standing there alongside them, living out his beliefs in the same (potentially ambiguous) place as them. And that would not, could not, have happened if I had sidled into an office, closed the door, and only then taken off my scarf and tightly buttoned coat.

So the next time you're sitting there in open plan cursing your lack of a "real" office, ask what the unexpected possibilities of being together with your fellow humans might be. There might just be something there. As Jacob said when he woke up from his dream: "Surely the Lord is in this place – and I did not know it!" Be prepared to be surprised.

7

The Annoying Colleague

Galatians 2:9–16 (NRSV)

[W]hen James and Cephas and John, who were acknowledged pillars, recognised the grace that had been given to me, they gave to Barnabas and me the right hand of fellowship, agreeing that we should go to the Gentiles and they to the circumcised. They asked only one thing, that we remember the poor, which was actually what I was eager to do. But when Cephas came to Antioch, I opposed him to his face, because he stood self-condemned; for until certain people came from James, he used to eat with the Gentiles. But after they came, he drew back and kept himself separate for fear of the circumcision faction. And the other Jews joined him in this hypocrisy, so that even Barnabas was led astray by their hypocrisy. But when I saw that they were not acting consistently with the truth of the gospel, I said to Cephas before them all, "If you, though a Jew, live like a Gentile and not like a Jew, how can you compel the Gentiles to live like Jews?" We ourselves are Jews by birth and not Gentile sinners; yet we know that a person is justified not by the works of the law but through faith in Jesus Christ.

So exactly how is your colleague annoying? The answer to that question is probably only constrained by the amount of time you have and by the limits of your imagination. They're too loud, or too quiet. They're too ambitious, or not ambitious enough. They work too hard, or they're lazy. They suck up to the boss, or they never show respect to anyone. They're always late and slacking, or always early and trying to show you up. They're far too gregarious, or they never mix enough. Or perhaps they fiddle their expenses, or never chip in the right amount for lunch, or they pass your ideas off as theirs. Perhaps they're always leering at people, or making inappropriate suggestions, or even sleeping around the office. Or they take it on themselves to lecture you about your failings, or set themselves up as the moral arbiter in the workplace, or start to "represent" you and your colleagues to your boss. As I said, how long do you have? The possibilities really are almost limitless. And given that, to return to the question of this section, where or what could be the godly potential of our annoying colleague?

I would imagine that you would expect me to talk about forgiveness, and/or the character-building benefits of being with and coping with someone who is deeply annoying. I'll touch on those briefly, but actually I want to start somewhere else. Some of you may know the American comic, George Carlin, who died a few years ago. Most of his routines are far too blue to be even vaguely repeatable in a religious book, so I'll have to summarize, but he did a brilliant one on driving. He talked about driving along the highway with all sorts of drivers, all of whom were, in one way or another, deeply annoying. Really, really, deeply annoying. The routine went on for some time, but at the end he summed the situation up like this: "Have you noticed how everyone on the road is a problem? There are all those maniacs who drive faster than you, and then all those idiots who drive slower. It's unbelievable!"

Never underestimate the power of humour to get to the heart of things. The point he was making was that we self-centred human beings judge everything around us solely, or certainly primarily, in relation to ourselves. For most of us, most of the time, we are the still centre around which the world spins. Everything is judged relative to us. We are the benchmark. Thus, in Carlin's comedy routine it doesn't much matter whether we're driving at 50, or 60, or 70 miles an hour. Those going faster than us will be the maniacs, and those going slower than us will be the idiots. There's nothing objective about it; it's just that, solely in relation to us, these people are faster or slower. Put slightly differently, they're annoying simply because they are different to us. And the logical, if slightly unsettling conclusion to be drawn from this is that, if indeed they are annoying to us, then it is entirely possible that we are annoying to them. In other words, bringing this back to the workplace, it is not beyond the realms of possibility that we might be the annoying colleague.

Take those pairs of opposites that I started off with. Someone who is too loud for us may be too quiet for someone else. Or we may seem too loud to them. Some people may think that we suck up to the boss too much, perhaps not as badly as Ms X or Mr Y, but still far too much. The person we regard as lazy may feel we're out to show them up. And still others – the ones that we think work too hard – may regard us as terrible slackers. Not everything is relative – but quite a lot is. So the first, and perhaps paradoxical, potential of the annoying colleague is to remind us how quick we are to judge, and how we do that judging often largely on the basis of regarding ourselves as the benchmark, the model, the gold standard for normal and appropriate behaviour. If we can reach this understanding – the realization that most people are annoying not on the basis of a truly objective standard, but simply because they are different to us – then a number of interesting, perhaps godly, things may follow from that.

The first is a little humility. If we realize that we are not perfect and everyone else imperfect – that we might have faults that others find annoying – then we will have re-learned an important lesson. If we assume that everyone else is wrong, then we have no incentive to improve our own behaviour because, almost by definition, our behaviour must be the norm. But if instead we start to question whether the colleague who annoys us is annoying us because that person is different (thereby opening up the possibility that we may also annoy them equally), then we are brought back to a place – because we are no longer "perfect" – where we can begin to grow again.

Second, and just as importantly, if there is the possibility that we are at fault, then that should make us less prone to judge others. Jesus, of course, tells us not to judge others. But not just – even though it's a good prudential argument – because we ourselves may similarly be judged. And not just because in judging we may unfairly condemn another, and then seek to impose punishment that is undeserved (and which it is not, in any event, our job to hand out). No, often the worst thing about judging is what it does to us. It makes us harder, harsher people. It makes us less able to relate to others as fellow humans. We see them instead as imperfect beings to be condemned. Judging makes us shrivel up inside. So, again, if our annoying colleague actually makes us realize that it could, in fact, be me (you) who is annoying, then that has real potential to re-open our lives. It could lift from us the self-imposed (if, sadly, enjoyable) burden of judging and enable us, instead, once again to relate to others as fellow humans, all of us imperfect, all of us struggling together in the world.

And, finally, leading on from that is the godly potential that flows from realizing that the difference that makes others annoying may actually be a positive advantage. We've looked a couple of times now at Paul's metaphor in 1 Corinthians about the church as a human body – and by extension in this section, to the body as a workplace. That collection becomes an entity, an organism, made up of separate parts that together make up a more valuable whole. But it's important to realize that part of the way that works – in a workplace, as in a church, or anywhere else – is not by some miraculous arrangement of perfectly harmonious people. It is likely, in fact, that all of those different Pauline skills together in one place will lead to conflicts if they're seen as challenging in any of the ways listed at the beginning. So the way to create harmony is to create a recognition of the value of difference, rather than the fake collegiality that so often shows up in the workplace. Looked at in this way, everyone brings something to the table – but it's something different. And the job of the boss, in particular, is to see where those skills fit in and to make everyone see the value of them. If you feel you're all pulling together, then whatever your differences, whatever your different ways of doing things, the annoyance factor drops way off because everyone is contributing to the same project, to the success of everyone.

So what does the Bible have to say? Jesus is quite vocal on this. As we've already discussed, "judge not, lest you be judged", as well as the Golden Rule, are obvious ones. "Do not try to take the speck out of someone else's eye before you remove the plank from your own" also seems highly relevant if we go back to the Carlin comedy skit. We tend to see ourselves as the model, when in fact we may be the problem. As I indicated at the beginning there is also the more traditional teaching on forgiving our enemies. There is the call for patience and forbearance in the face of those who annoy us, or worse: "If anyone strikes you on the right cheek, turn the other also". And, of course, "Love your enemies and pray for those who persecute you"; "Forgive your brother not seven times but seventy times seven."

Now all these are helpful, necessary even, for recognizing

some of the potential that we've been talking about. Fostering an awareness that we may not always be right. Reminding us of the need to curb our own judgmental instincts, of the need not to respond even to genuine provocation with anger or force because of the ratcheting up in conflict to which that will lead. Doing all of that will, without doubt, make us better people. But I do also think that they sound like counsels of perfection, possibly even a little preachy.

So I want to consider another story from the Bible – our passage from Galatians – that illustrates this in a more human way and which opens up another possibility: the possibility that the sometimes annoying colleague may be placed in the workplace to spur necessary change. That promoting disharmony may actually get people asking the right questions. It may be uncomfortable, it may upset the routine, but it may also make us think again and ask ourselves what God wants from us.

Exhibit A in this category is Paul. Even if he counsels us not to let the sun go down on our anger, he himself often managed to pack an awful lot of anger into the day itself. His letter to the Galatians, from which our story comes, is an extended, enraged attack on other followers of the Way – his colleagues! – who were telling the Galatians that they could only be proper Christians if they followed the strict Jewish ritual laws on food, circumcision, and so on. Rubbish, says Paul – dead wrong, absolute junk! It's about what comes from God, and what goes on in our hearts, not whether something's been snipped off. And this was to people supposedly on the same team – if not in the same office, then at least in the same company.

The most famous of his dust-ups was with his close and, arguably, senior colleague, Peter in Antioch. Paul has already been to Jerusalem, to the Council, to get agreement that circumcision is not necessary (even though not everyone agreed with that). But there is still the issue of the food laws. Peter comes to Antioch and eats with the Gentiles – until, that is, some of the hardliners show up from Jerusalem. And suddenly Peter pulls back and no longer eats with the unclean. "Well!!" says Paul in his letter to the Galatians, "I wasn't having ANY of that, so I pointed out his gross HYPOCRISY to him in public; in front of EVERYONE!!!!!" One can only imagine what Peter thought and felt. But the point is that Paul was right, and God was working through him. We are justified by faith, and by faith alone. Without Paul and his mission to the Gentiles, without his generous extension of fellowship to people very different to himself – but who accepted Christ – Christianity would today simply be another footnote amidst a crowd of first-century footnotes.

So another potential of our annoying colleague is to alert us to the uncomfortable, but growth-enhancing, possibilities of change. It's not just about humility on our part, but also an acceptance that change, although unsettling, will keep us, and our faith, alive and growing. It can be very difficult, and conflict should not be the norm, but we must be open to the possibility.

I want, finally, to come back to a slightly more traditional way of looking at this – the command to forgive, and so on – but from a slightly different angle. One of my favourite quotes is from Henry Wadsworth Longfellow, who said, "My enemy is the person whose story I have not heard." Just think about that for a second. If someone else is an object, a two-dimensional cardboard cut-out about whom we know almost nothing, then it's easy to hate them, to judge them, even to destroy them. But once we talk to them, once we hear their story, they become a person very much like us: a bundle of emotions, fears, hopes, dreams, hurts, oddities, vanities, virtues. And it is much harder then to hate, judge or destroy them.

Most of the things that I've talked about so far, while completely valid, are of benefit either to us or to our annoying colleague, but not necessarily to both of us. Hearing the other person's story, however, changes things. If we seek to get past their "annoyingness" by trying to hear their story, by trying to find out what makes them tick, then we will have started to build a relationship that is not just us, and not just them, but is both of us. Perhaps, ideally, we get to understand them so well, and they us, that the source of the annoyance disappears. But even if it doesn't, or doesn't completely, we will have started to build something godly – another relationship as intended by God who created us to be in relationship with both Him and with our fellow beings as part of that healing of creation. So we should make it our job to know those around us whose stories we have not heard. And that is particularly true of the person who could most easily be our enemy in the workplace if we delve no deeper than the surface – our annoying colleague.

8

The New Arrival

Mark 6:7–13 (NRSV)

He called the twelve and began to send them out two by two, and gave them authority over the unclean spirits. He ordered them to take nothing for their journey except a staff; no bread, no bag, no money in their belts; but to wear sandals and not to put on two tunics. He said to them, "Wherever you enter a house, stay there until you leave the place. If any place will not welcome you and they refuse to hear you, as you leave, shake off the dust that is on your feet as a testimony against them." So they went out and proclaimed that all should repent. They cast out many demons, and anointed with oil many who were sick and cured them.

I haven't actually changed jobs for almost fifteen years now, although I did move back from the US to the UK, and the shape of my job has changed almost totally over that time. But, occasionally, I get glimpses of what it's like to be the new arrival. I join new committees or groups; I start new initiatives. But the only time I really come close to that feeling of being the new arrival is when I travel to somewhere that I've never been before. A few years ago I went to Buenos Aires. I left a cold, grey London in January and arrived in a 90-degree southern summer. I spent an afternoon walking around in bright sun and deep shade before my meetings began. I had a map but no real idea where I was, no sense of the bigger shape of the city. Some things looked very familiar, others very foreign. I didn't speak Spanish, and I had no local currency. No one knew me, and I knew no one. No one had any preconceptions about me, and I had none about anyone I saw. I walked, and walked, and walked. And as I did that, I began to see beyond the cares, and concerns, and work of the present moment; the weight of things done and not done; the obligations of the coming days, weeks, months. I began to see beyond all those – to a possibility where my life could be lived day by day, not constantly, anxiously, scanning the horizon, but looking at what was right in front of me; of making decisions on which fork in the road to take today – not some point in the future – based not on a map or a plan but on what looked most interesting, most promising. Of course, eventually I got back to my hotel and slipped back into my "real" life of meetings and work plans and timelines. But for a moment – for a few hours – I had a tantalizing glimpse of what a differently lived life might be.

And that is what I remember of starting a new job. Other than a brief interview and some references, you were unknown. Your story was a blank slate upon which you could write afresh. There were new relationships to be developed, a new reputation to make. New interests to be pursued, and new specialisms to be built up. And there was the chance to put the past in the past – to learn from old mistakes that in this new place no one would hold against you. To bring enthusiasm and freshness and new ideas to this new place.

But, of course, my experience has been that those feelings are more welcomed in some places than others. If the workplace is well run, if people know they're pulling together and that they are valued for what they are, then the new arrival may be welcomed. But if the workplace is already divided, the new arrival may be seen as a threat, more like a bacteria to be attacked by the body's defences. I've seen that too – more reminiscent of the *Lord of the Flies* than anything else. (Although, and not for the first time in these chapters, we can also easily recognize that same problem in churches of which we may have been members.)

So what is the godly potential of the new arrival? Is it just that freshness which quickly fades to cynicism in the face of time-serving colleagues, an uncaring boss, and tiring, boring, repetitive tasks? That brief moment? Or is there more? Well, I think there is more. Some of the points are obvious, but some are a little more difficult to disentangle.

Let me start with the more obvious ones. Regardless of how functional or dysfunctional our workplace is, new arrivals are in need of help. And that is an opportunity for us as well as them. The physical ones may seem straightforward, but they shouldn't be overlooked. In the first place where I worked – which was a little on the dysfunctional side – the bank manager had told me by phone to show up at 8.20 in the morning. So I did. But in the following weeks I couldn't work out why I kept getting dirty looks (other than the obvious fact that I was British and they weren't) when I showed up each day at 8.20. Only after four weeks did someone tell me that the start time was 15 minutes earlier, at 8.05. It would have been a kindness to have been told that on Day Two.

Another obvious area of help is letting people know where the real bear traps are. What are the red lines that shouldn't be crossed? What is it that really infuriates the boss? Who are the notoriously difficult people? Of course, we should do this lightly, and not with the intention of scaring the new arrival, or for that matter with the intent of recruiting them into our faction. But to shield the new arrival from obvious harm is good. Yet, too often, we let people wander into trouble – or even worse encourage it to cheer ourselves up, or something.

A slightly different form of help is enabling the new arrival to develop their skills. Instead of just putting the person in an office, telling them to get on with it, and shutting the door, we can actively train them – give them practical tips, or technical advice, whether informally or through formal training. Again this shouldn't be heavy-handed, but there were several times in my early career when I wished that somebody had taken me under their wing and taught me the basics. And this also relates to another aspect of what we talked about when we looked at the team. The team will be more effective overall if the skill levels of the newest arrivals are higher rather than lower. It's that straightforward. But so often we leave new arrivals alone to "get on with the job" when even minimal direction would greatly improve their work and thereby improve the overall performance (and, thus, godly potential) of the team.

Another, subtly different, form of help could come from mentoring – again whether formal or informal. Mentoring isn't training in a formal sense; it's more of a walking alongside someone. Sharing experiences, thoughts, a life outlook. Showing empathy that helps others deal with issues at work or at home. Improving the quality of life in the workplace. It's a two-way thing that helps both mentee and mentor. So there are lots of opportunities for us to help the new arrival – to help our neighbour.

But it's the intriguing, apparently ephemeral, fleeting, idea of freshness that I want to return to. It seems it can never last, but we do need to ask what effect it has both on the new arrival and on the established members of the workplace, and also ask whether that "freshness", if beneficial, can be refreshed or re-created. As for the effect on the new arrival, I did touch on that at the beginning: that feeling of so many possibilities, of not being burdened with a past that people always judge and measure us by, of a desire to explore and bring new ideas, and of approaching new people without preconceptions.

But what about the established members of the workplace? For them, it can be viewed as a challenge: someone younger than they are, possibly with better qualifications, with youthful energy which seems to show those older established workers up. However, it can also be a breath of fresh air, something that reminds them of the possibilities of the place, of what it could be. Something that reminds them of what they could be. Something that gives them – even momentarily – more energy and hope. Something that makes them look at their work, or an aspect of it, in a new way – a new angle on it, a slightly different way of doing it. And it can also be – excitingly – the lifting of a burden of responsibility, of the accretion of tasks, and of relationships, and of mistakes; the momentary wiping clean of the slate that refreshes the soul.

The Bible has quite a lot to say on new arrivals. From the Old Testament, the treatment of guests, of the new, honoured stranger can be analogized to the new arrival in the workplace. The new person is not someone to be shunned but someone to be welcomed. There are also many examples of training and nurturing the new arrival. The New Testament also talks about this, both in terms of welcoming strangers and also the obligation to one's neighbour. But equally interesting in relation to the last aspect that we mentioned, that of bringing fresh air into the workplace, is some of what Jesus has to say about not being burdened by worries. The passage from Mark's Gospel about the Twelve being sent out on their own for the first time captures that immediacy, that lack of burden, all the opportunities in front of them. They weren't to worry about clothes or food or lodging. That would just happen. The point was to go out and exercise their new ministry today – joyfully, uncomplicatedly.

Jesus often worries that in our concern to prepare for tomorrow we will miss today. We'll miss the opportunity to focus on God, because we will be so focused on material needs – hence the teaching on not worrying about tomorrow, on not worrying about what we are to eat or what we are to wear (Matthew 6:25–34). All that will be provided. In a literal sense this is always hard to take, because obviously we do have to worry a little about tomorrow – many of us have mortgages, and pensions, and children, and elderly parents to worry about – and we do have to work to live. But the point is broader than that – it's about not being trapped by expectations, by fears, whatever. It's about regaining freedom of current action, enjoying, benefitting from the current moment.

Another parable that well illustrates this is the one about the bigger barns (Luke 12:16–21). In this story, an already successful landowner is blessed with still greater abundance. His barns are already filled to capacity with his existing produce, so he rubs his hands together as he speculates how long all this will last him, and he begins to make plans for building still bigger barns in which to store his still greater harvest. But even as he does this he is visited by God who tells him that his life will be taken that very same night. Now this can be seen as a parable about a lack of gratitude, about not thanking God, about an obsession with human issues, about a failure to spread the fruits of our good fortune. But it can also be read to be about a failure of imagination, about a concern with tomorrow that prevents us from seeing the possibilities of today. If we go into the workplace every day trapped by fears about what may happen, or go in determined to do the same as we did yesterday, only more so, then we lose the possibility of seeing things afresh. Life, our job, everything, simply becomes a continuum where the present is just a minuscule point on a line dominated almost entirely by the past and by the future.

Seen in that way, the present offers very little opportunity, either as a time to be enjoyed for what it is or as something which holds the possibility for a new departure, for new possibilities – possibilities led by God, rather than by our own concern for preparations for a future that may never come.

To make, and possibly belabour, the point just one more time: part of our dissatisfaction with work comes from the idea that we are stuck in a rut, in a routine that makes every day the same on a forced march from past to future. But if we realize that each day actually holds real possibilities for something new, for a new way of looking at things or doing things, then it is no longer routine. So how do we recapture that freshness? That sense of possibility?

I talked before about the lifting of a burden which allows us to enjoy the present moment. That is the elusive freshness we need to recapture. And yet that refreshment doesn't necessarily require a recreation of the past (when we were young and hopeful…), but rather a reimagining of the present. And that reimagining may be as simple as remembering and then accepting the gift of forgiveness that God offers us every day – the freshness that can come from renewing our relationship with God. Now, again, there is a danger of that sounding preachy or pious, but the remarkable fact is that with God we are never stuck in a rut and never trapped in the past. There can be a real renewal from taking off our sins, our past failures, whatever we want to call them, and putting them in the hands of God. By realizing (or remembering) that, we may be able to recreate the freshness, the lightness of spirit. And if we do this, we can ourselves become again (and again) the new arrival.

So the new arrival can – like the new disciples sent out by Jesus – teach us, or remind us, to try to live in the present moment, to live for what God has given us today. If we try to imagine what today may hold, rather than next week, next month, next year, we can live more satisfied lives oriented towards God. Unburdened by regrets of the past or fears of the future, we may again see new opportunities, new possibilities in the workplace.

9

Retirement

Numbers 8:21–26 (NIV)

The Levites purified themselves and washed their clothes. Then Aaron presented them as a wave offering before the Lord and made atonement for them to purify them. After that, the Levites came to do their work at the Tent of Meeting under the supervision of Aaron and his sons. They did with the Levites just as the Lord commanded Moses. The Lord said to Moses, "This applies to the Levites: Men twenty-five years old or more shall come to take part in the work at the Tent of Meeting, but at the age of fifty, they must retire from their regular service and work no longer. They may assist their brothers in performing their duties at the Tent of Meeting, but they themselves must not do the work. This, then, is how you are to assign the responsibilities of the Levites."

Not that I was counting or anything, but as I forced my way onto a crowded and damp London Underground train on the day that I first gave this chapter as a talk, it didn't completely escape my notice that in exactly eight years and ten months my company pension would vest, and that I could pack away my tax books forever and move off into the golden decades of golf and travel… Well, in fact, I have something different planned, but I do have colleagues who know the company pension scheme back to front and really are counting the days. Even if it's years and years away, the size of the vested pension and any executive top-up seems to be what keeps them going through the day. If only I work for another X years, they seem to say, everything will be all right; somehow this will all have been worthwhile. And then there are others for whom retirement is not even to be countenanced. Why? Because they enjoy their jobs so much? Something about a feeling of continuing usefulness as we become older? Something to do with the status that a good job confers? All of the above? Quite possibly.

What is clear is that retirement is a subject about which no one over fifty – perhaps even forty-five – is neutral. And that's important for the workplace, because quite often those people are the leaders of today. Their frame of mind, their outlook, will have a significant impact on the way the business functions and feels. And really, there is nothing more miserable than people hanging on with no interest in their jobs in order to reach a magic number at which they can cash it all in. Dead man walking. Nor, however, is it ideal when people, however much they love their jobs, stay around as their abilities begin to fade and their successors queue up. Both will have negative effects on those around them. So, having said all that, we need to ask ourselves the usual question. What about retirement might be transformative? But I also want to do more than that and take a different angle on this topic by asking whether the traditional view of retirement may actually be ungodly.

Perhaps before we go there, however, I do also need to acknowledge that there may, of course, be other reasons why people do not have a choice about retirement. Those reasons have less to do with a decision about leaving or not leaving the workplace than they do with a simple lack of choice. Some may just not be able to afford to retire because they would no longer be able to support someone dependent on them. For others it would mean having to move from where they live and from their community. For others still, it would mean the loss of the only friends or human interaction that they have. These people are not hanging on for the pension or because they love the job; they're hanging on because there is no real alternative.

But whether it's those who can't wait to leave or those who feel they can't, this can have profound impact upon the workplace. At a very obvious level, it can depress the people who do actually want to be there. But there are other ways in which it might also impact that godly potential of the workplace. To look at those, I'd like to revisit some of the theology of work that we touched on in the first few chapters. Martin Luther, you may remember, had a doctrine of vocations (or "stations"), whereby God had called us to the place where we found ourselves, and every vocation was to be regarded as equally honourable. Unhappy work is a negation of that. It clearly says to your fellow workers – and to God – I am not happy to be in this place, but I have no choice. And you may also remember that we looked at Miroslav Volf, who updated Luther's doctrine by allowing for a spirit-led determination as to what our true vocation might be. Through participation in the healing of God's creation in the work to which the Spirit has led us, we reach our full potential. Well, again, if we're not doing what we think is our highest calling, we are unlikely to be participating – or, at least, participating fully – in God's ongoing work on earth. And that should give us pause. I'm not saying that we shouldn't make sensible provision for the future, or indeed worry a little about what that future might hold. But to put ourselves in shackles – be they made of iron or gold – for a future which may never come, seems, to put it mildly, a real shame.

So what's the answer? Well, I think that part of the problem lies in the binary nature of modern retirement. One day you're working; the next day you're not. One day you may have the status and a grand title; the next you don't. One day you have the pay packet; the next day you don't. One day you have a ready-made group to fit into and interact with; the next day you don't. This cliff-edge effect makes retirement scary and unattractive for many – and, yes, for some, also impossible. Yet something's wrong with that picture. As we've discussed before, God intends us to live lives integrated from day to day between work and the rest of our lives. They're not in two (or more) separate compartments. By the same token, however, if work is as important for God and the kingdom as Luther and Volf think it is, then neither is work something that happens just between the ages of twenty and sixty-five (any more than God is only around on a Sunday morning between 10.00 and 11.30). Properly thought of, work starts well before we reach twenty and should go on long after we pass sixty-five. We all have something to contribute to the kingdom. The key is that that contribution will always be in proportion to our ability – not just to our ability, however, but also to our energy and our strength, and to our other circumstances. A man of sixty-five may not have the physical strength of a man of thirty; a woman of sixty-five may not have the same energy levels as one of thirty. But the people of sixty-five do have just as much to offer – simply not the same.

So – and here the godly potential may begin to get clearer – what this argues for is a view of work that is not a progression in a career from success to success over forty years until some slightly arbitrary point is reached at which the lights get turned off. Rather, different jobs should be regarded as age-appropriate and equally valuable to God – even, perhaps, if not equally remunerated in earthly money. A recent study showed that younger workers had more energy and more stamina, but that older workers had greater experience which enabled them to make decisions based on judgment. Why can't we expand this insight a little? There doesn't have to be a rigid framework. People should be able to move through the phases of a job making moves between certain types of work at different points. Thought of in this way, a company may well have many things for seventy-year-olds to do.

So what does the Bible have to say on this? Well directly, not that much. The opening reading from Numbers is unusual. But it does directly address the issue. The Levites are to work at the Tent of Meeting – that is, the central part of the tabernacle where the holy objects were kept – from the ages of twenty-five to fifty. At fifty they are to help the younger Levites in their tasks, not to perform the main work itself. In other words, they were to retire from the main work, but crucially, they were not to leave completely; they were to carry on assisting. That's it, however, for direct scriptural application.

However, to the other point that we talked about – dropping the cares of work and cruising off into a twenty-year sunset of golf and 6 p.m. cocktails – I want to return to the parable of the bigger barns that we looked at in the previous chapter. As you'll remember, the wealthy landowner, already blessed with abundance in his crops, is then blessed with even more. So he decides to tear down his current barns, and build even bigger ones so that he can store this new abundance. Then, he thinks (secure in the knowledge that his future is provided for), he will be able to relax, and, in the words of the parable, "eat, drink and be merry" – except, of course, that God then shows up and tells him that he will die that night. In the last chapter we talked about this in terms of living in the present moment, of not ignoring that time in favour of the (hypothetical) future. But, as I am sure you can easily see, this might also be a parable about retirement. If our role in God's creation is to work and somehow contribute to its ongoing improvement, then storing all of its abundance for ourselves to provide for a time when we no longer have to contribute to creation may not in fact be part of God's great plan. The parable suggests that the abundance should, at least in part, be distributed to others, and the landowner carry on working with God to produce more.

Now, I want to be a bit careful, and I think I certainly need to make clear that I am not necessarily talking about labouring away in the same workplace you've always been in until the day you drop. (There really are very few people on their deathbed who wish they'd spent more time in the office.) But there are many other kinds of work, whether it's volunteering at church or a hospital, working part-time in a shop, helping to run a sports club, or being involved in a voluntary organization or a charity. But this book is mostly about the for-profit workplace, so that's where I'll focus.

Let's come back to the idea of the Levites retiring. They take a step backwards, to be sure, but don't step completely away. What effect might that have on a workplace? Well, it could be quite dramatic. If you could retain the wisdom and experience of some of the older members of the organization, while at the same time bringing some of the more energetic younger members into leadership positions, then that could be to the benefit of the whole business. But it might also require us to reimagine the way the workplace works. The key is dealing with the issue of status and, more particularly, the loss of status. Can we reimagine the workplace so that while it still needs lines of responsibility, needs people who "own" projects, and needs people who can drive things forward, it also can allow for moves between those roles that don't result in a loss of status? That really would embody Luther's idea of vocation – that every role is good in the sight of God. We would have to figure out how this interacts with tricky issues such as compensation, but wouldn't the workplace work better if those best suited to certain roles filled them and then vacated them when they were no longer suited to them – but yet still had the ability to retain a valued place whether full- or part-time within the workplace? And indeed, wouldn't we all be better off if we didn't confuse who we were with a grand job title? Too many times I have seen people captured by what they think their job title says about them.

Just for once, my slightly disparaged US legal background may provide a model. In many UK law firms, especially in the City of London, you'll hardly see anybody much past fifty-five or even fifty in several of the largest firms. Some combination of massive enrichment and complete exhaustion pushes them out. But if you go to the many US law firms, even very big ones, you'll find several partners in their sixties, seventies, and even eighties. That may not be your cup of tea, but it adds something to the firm. They are the institutional memory; they have decades of experience and judgment that can help solve seemingly novel problems; they can have time to help junior lawyers when the mainstream partners are just too busy; and they can also – occasionally – hold back their more aggressive younger colleagues. Like the older Levites, they may no longer be partners – they may have some title like "of counsel" – but they add something to the firm and encourage their fellows to step out of full partnership even if they don't want to leave the firm. Now there are plenty of other problems with law firms, but in this respect, at least, there is the possibility of the ladder touching down. Of people continuing in some way, regardless of their age, to contribute – even at a law firm – to the work of God's creation. By the assignment of roles according to ability and energy and experience. By discarding traditional notions of status, so that the movement between roles becomes fluid, easy, to the benefit of everyone, rather than up, up, up, and then suddenly out.

If we can find more flexible ways to keep people in the workforce, then where we work would be a better place, and we might all be better workers. The death of the company pension may be pushing the private sector in that direction, but nothing is more miserable and less godly than unhappy, bored, unmotivated workers wasting the days and months and years of their lives until they can clock off. So, to counter this, let's not view retirement as a cliff over which we must jump or be pushed, but rather a transition from one form of working to another, from one job to another. By all means a shift to less work or, at least, less strenuous work, but still a place where we can have a part in God's ongoing creation and where we keep ourselves mentally and physically active, involved, and fulfilled. A pipe dream? Perhaps, but it can happen, and if it does the godly possibilities of this transition will suddenly appear in front of us.

10

The P45
(or "Pink Slip")

Job 38:1–13 (NIV)

Then the Lord answered Job out of the storm. He said: "Who is this that obscures my counsel with words without knowledge? Brace yourself like a man; I will question you, and you shall answer me. Where were you when I laid the earth's foundation? Tell me, if you understand. Who marked off its dimensions? Surely you know! Who stretched a measuring line across it? On what were its footings set, or who laid its cornerstone – while the morning stars sang together and all the angels shouted for joy? Who shut up the sea behind doors when it burst forth from the womb, when I made the clouds its garment and wrapped it in thick darkness, when I fixed limits for it and set its doors and bars in place, when I said, 'This far you may come and no farther; here is where your proud waves halt'? Have you ever given orders to the morning, or shown the dawn its place, that it might take the earth by the edges and shake the wicked out of it?"

once gave a talk at work as part of a mentoring programme. My first slide showed my CV (US: "résumé"), which I had helpfully colour coded. The purpose of those colours was to deconstruct what appeared to be an incredibly coherent, well-planned career, presumably set in train with relentless single-mindedness by me at about the age of thirteen. I persuaded them that it wasn't that coherent (or any of those other things). Red, less than half the chart, signified things that I had planned to do in advance of doing them. Green, almost half, signified opportunities that I had grabbed as they came along. But one of the entries was surrounded by a jagged black line. That, as I explained to them, signified something that had gone badly wrong – something that was, without doubt, the low point of my professional life. I still remember very well sitting in a partner's office at my law firm for my annual review and getting the news that my career at that firm was effectively at an end. I hadn't seen it coming (although I hadn't exactly been enjoying myself either). I was meant to have had formal notice before the review meeting of what was coming, but it had been so obliquely delivered that I still hadn't twigged why the partner who had given me the black mark had come and sat in my office for fifteen minutes talking in the broadest generalities about the difficulties of practising law. So I sat there during my review, feeling like a spectator at a rather bizarre play in which I – disembodied – was one of the principal characters. And as I did, I caught sight of a poster on the wall. It was for the local production of a play based on the Dickens novel *A Tale of Two Cities*. And there in large, bold letters was the famous opening quote: "It was the best of times; it was the worst of times." Well, I thought to myself, that's half true.

It was a horrible time, and it changed me in ways that I'm still working out today. But I can also say with absolute assurance that it was one of the best things that ever happened to me professionally – without a shadow of a doubt. My father was a very successful lawyer, who'd made a brilliant career at a single firm over forty years. After one half-hearted attempt at university not to be a lawyer, I had succumbed and entered a world to which, especially on the US side of the Atlantic, I was spectacularly ill-suited, both by skills and by temperament. And yet I had no idea what else to do, so I drifted. If I hadn't hit that wall so hard during the review – which might have been the case in a more forgiving firm – then I might still be wearily dragging myself into a law office, and (as we discussed in relation to retirement in the previous chapter) counting not just the years and the months, but the days and the minutes until retirement became possible. Perhaps I could have been trained up to perform better; perhaps some mentoring might have helped. But, at best, that would only marginally have improved what would have still remained a classic case of a round peg in a square hole.

Now I wouldn't wish this experience on anyone (although many of you reading this will also have experienced it, or something like it), but I would be the first to admit that, under those circumstances, I was relatively fortunate. I was going to be able to find another job of some type, my wife, Michelle, was still working, and our financial and family obligations were pretty manageable. There will be those for whom this is an absolute disaster – they won't be able to pay for their housing; it will precipitate the final argument that leads to the divorce; it may bring on depression. So I'm not going to blithely say that it's always a blessing in disguise because, as Winston Churchill is reputed to have said, sometimes the blessing may be very well disguised indeed. But in my case, at that point in my life, it was truly a blessing. And I believe it can be more often than it might appear for others too. It was for me the place where the ladder suddenly became apparent – a ladder I was then able to climb up to get out of a particularly difficult hole.

But first we do need to acknowledge and deal with the trauma. In the same way that the Victorians dressed up death from a full wardrobe of euphemisms – passed over to the other side, fallen asleep, resting in the Lord, and so on – we do the same for getting the sack. We talk about people exploring other opportunities, spending more time with their families, right-sizing, letting go, and taking a mid-career break. But nothing can blunt the immediate pain for the recipient of the P45/pink slip because it is as simple and as fundamental as being told that you are not wanted.

I'll talk about this some more in a moment. But we should also spare a thought for the person delivering the bad news. We tend to have an image of a heartless Victorian plutocrat or perhaps, slightly updated, someone like Mr Burns in *The Simpsons*, happily slashing and burning their way through department after department. But, in fact, most bosses and HR people hate sacking people. Maybe they're having to break up a team they've spent time and effort assembling, or maybe they're having to admit they made a hiring mistake. Perhaps the one being fired is someone who gets very emotional or someone who becomes abusive. It's almost never easy for either side.

So what is the godly potential of the P45 for the workplace? I'll return to my own story at the end, but I do want to deal with a number of other possibilities, while all the time emphasizing, again and again, that for many people being fired appears to be an event with no possible upside or potential. I do think, however, that there are several potentially beneficial effects. Two relate to the workplace as a whole, and then others to some of the individuals involved. The first is pretty obvious – although, in fact, the P45/pink slip is actually handed out perhaps less in these circumstances than it should be. There are some people who disrupt a workplace and harm the atmosphere. Perhaps they are bullies, perhaps they are dishonest, perhaps their behaviour is inappropriate, perhaps they are bone idle. In all of those cases, if efforts to change their behaviour are unsuccessful, then they probably ought to go. It's bad for the other people there. And, far from there being an obligation to keep on people like that to give them yet one more chance, in fact there's a real obligation to get rid of them for the benefit of others in the workplace individually, and as a team.

A second case relates to instances when the person isn't up to the job, which means that it gets done badly, and either the business suffers or his or her fellow workers have to do that person's job in addition to their own. Again, that creates stress and tension and is, in the end, simply not fair on the others. But this usually requires more thought and careful handling than the first case. I work for GE, and the CEO when I joined was the legendary American boss, Jack Welch. He had a number of well-known management techniques, and one of them was that the bottom 10 per cent of performers had to go each year.

Now, it didn't work quite like that. There were performance plans to allow for improvement before anything happened, and I'm fairly certain it was also generally less than 10 per cent. But the rationale was this: it's clear that you've been put into a position above your capabilities, and while that's not good for the business, in fact it's not good for you either, because you're constantly worried and stressed, feeling you're letting people down and getting no job satisfaction. So, go find a job to which you are suited, and enjoy your life. Now while this sounds like cynical dressing-up of a need to get rid of people for economic reasons, or because you don't like them, actually it has considerable resonance with at least the thrust of what Miroslav Volf says about finding the job to which we are truly suited in order to best serve God. So, the corollary of that might be that if we're in a job beyond our capabilities, then in addition to disadvantaging ourselves, we are also disadvantaging God. I'm not going to syllogistically jump from that to saying that Jack Welch was the agent of God, but, properly done, moving people away from jobs to which they are not suited towards those to which they are can improve not just the workplace but also the life of the individual who gets the P45.

But the key lies in those words "properly done". And that's where the potential expands to also touch the people responsible for the firing. From my own experience at the wrong end of this, I can certainly offer a few tips on how not to do it. But there is actually the potential in the experience for the person doing the firing also to grow – and possibly for the rest of the workplace. Often the temptation is just to "get it over with", and we probably all know people who have been fairly brutally escorted off the premises with a cardboard box of their possessions, having had their security pass removed. In other cases it's hideously drawn out, with lots of half-conversations and oblique references, in the hope that the target will get the idea and quit – but with no one prepared finally to pull the trigger.

The godly potential lies in treating this as something that might genuinely be to the advantage of a person not suited to the job from which they're being fired. Obviously, that requires empathy with the person involved – the fears and concerns they are going to have. It equally involves being honest about why that person doesn't have the skill set needed, but also what skills they do have and in what jobs those skills might work. If there are other opportunities within the firm for those gifts, then that should be explored – as should the potential loss of status that we talked about in the previous chapter. If there are not opportunities inside the business, then the company should offer outplacement services (and I do mean proper outplacement services) to help that person find a new job. Severance pay should be generous enough to ease any immediate fears. But the main thing is not to do what so often happens. In order to cover up a bad hiring decision or a bad promotion decision, people are told that it's all their fault – that they're subpar; that they've failed. So the separation is fatally botched – it becomes emotional, negative, wounding. Clearly there are employment law reasons why certain things have to be said and done in certain ways – and these might make the process feel a lot less human. Nevertheless, honesty and empathy in this process can turn it from being something unremittingly awful into something which, while difficult, holds some potential for change, for growth.

So what does the Bible have to say about this? Well, as often, not that much directly. However, the Bible does have a lot to say about change – often unpleasant, unsettling change – and also a lot to say about changes in status. Both of those themes appear in the Old Testament story of Job. Job, a good and successful man, had everything taken from him in a series of tests. He was then confronted by a series of friends, who told him in no uncertain terms that it was his fault. Job kept believing in himself and in God, although he raged at God for what had happened. And God, eventually, gives the magisterial answer that I have quoted at start of the chapter. "Job," He says, "you simply can't know everything that's going on – you must trust." Job does trust, and eventually all is made right again. So while that pain and sudden removal of so much taken for granted is deeply unsettling, the message from Job's story is to hang in there and trust in God.

Another relevant loss of status in the Old Testament involves a whole people. In the generations after Joseph, the Israelites in Egypt were gradually enslaved, until all their freedom was gone. Under the leadership of Moses, however, they decide to end this. Despite their uncertainty and fear about quitting Egypt, they decide to walk away from the job to something better. Of course, the route to the land of milk and honey lay through the desert and considerable testing, but, in the end, the journey was worthwhile. There will be times when we feel like Job and others when, like the Israelites, we feel abused in (and yet fearful of leaving) our current job. In both cases, however, we have to put our faith in something better coming along, even if that seems impossible at the time.

Now, of course, that's all very well, and nothing that I've said deals with a situation like a mass lay-off in a bankruptcy. It may be that it works out well for some, but for others it is utter devastation. There I can offer little comfort – other, again, than the story of Job. Sometimes we just don't know why things happen, but we shouldn't blame ourselves in that situation, but keep going, keep trusting.

I want to finish with the postscript to the story that I started with. I was under no pressure to leave immediately, but I decided not to stick around. So in my mentoring talk, the next move on my CV was circled in blue – and what that signified was a job that had allowed me to recoup and recover. It was something that many people regarded as a lower status job compared with one in a prestigious law firm. But for me, again, it was one of the best things I ever did. It laid the foundation for everything else that I've been able to do since. But much more importantly, at the time, it allowed me a period to recover. There was interesting work, some proper training, and a much less pressured working environment. Yes, less money, less status, but much more enjoyment and a chance to rebuild my confidence. And without what had effectively been a P45, that wouldn't have happened. I'd have soldiered on. I'd have stayed in Washington. I'd probably never have got ordained.

I don't believe in a God who has a big book with our lives already fully planned out in it. I do, however, believe that God occasionally intervenes in ways we cannot understand and that may even seem painful at the time, but that turn out for the best. That for me was the godly potential in all that, the place where – at least in retrospect – it was clear that heaven had touched earth. To be sure, as I've said again and again, a P45 can (almost certainly will) feel horrible at the time. But if we continue to believe in ourselves (and in God) then something good may come of it. It may turn out to be the beginning of the end of exile. We may have some time in the desert first, but at the other end something better, something of God, may be waiting.

PART II

Where is God at Work in Work's Dilemmas?

11

What Happens If... I Face an Ethical Dilemma at Work?

Acts 17:16–25, 32 (NRSV)

While Paul was waiting for them in Athens, he was deeply distressed to see that the city was full of idols. So he argued in the synagogue with the Jews and the devout persons, and also in the marketplace every day with those who happened to be there. Also some Epicurean and Stoic philosophers debated with him. Some said, "What does this babbler want to say?" Others said, "He seems to be a proclaimer of foreign divinities." (This was because he was telling the good news about Jesus and the resurrection.) So they took him and brought him to the Areopagus and asked him, "May we know what this new teaching is that you are presenting? It sounds rather strange to us, so we would like to know what it means." Now all the Athenians and the foreigners living there would spend their time in nothing but telling or hearing something new. Then Paul stood in front of the Areopagus and said, "Athenians, I see how extremely religious you are in every way. For as I went through the city and looked carefully at the objects of your worship, I found among them an altar with the inscription, 'To an unknown god.' What therefore you worship as unknown, this I proclaim to you. The God who made the world

and everything in it, he who is Lord of heaven and earth, does not
live in shrines made by human hands, nor is he served by human
hands, as though he needed anything, since he himself gives to all
mortals life and breath and all things... When they heard of the
resurrection of the dead, some scoffed; but others said, "We will
hear you again about this."

Having looked in Part I at those "structural" features of the workplace, the way an office or workplace is set up, and the challenges and opportunities that can lead to, in this second section I want to look at a different aspect of the workplace. I want to look at those times in the workplace when we have to make decisions on difficult issues, on dilemmas, that may reveal to us something about God in that place, about God in our lives, and about God's purpose for us. As much as in the structures of the workplace, it is also in the facing and resolution of dilemmas that God may unexpectedly become apparent. Sometimes in those dilemmas the possibility of the ladder coming down from heaven in the most unpromising place may suddenly become clear.

Before getting to those dilemmas, those difficult decisions, however, in this introductory chapter I want to look at the mechanics of how we make those decisions. Because it is not just in the decisions themselves, but in the way they are made, that their godly potential may lie. Every day we face decisions large and small, some very obvious, some almost invisible. But how do we approach those decisions? Consciously or unconsciously? After deep thought and analysis, or intuitively? As I'll go on to explain, most of our daily decisions are taken unconsciously, intuitively. For that to lead to good outcomes, however, there needs to be a framework, an environment which trains and sustains us. Let's start, therefore, with a broad-brush (and brief) outline of what that ethical (and Christian) framework might look like.

* * *

"Ethics" is obviously a key word, but it's not always well defined. Despite some disagreement, I think it differs from the word "morality", at least in common usage. Morality is about commands and has come to mean something rather primal, often viscerally judgmental. Ethics is something a little more structured; less about commands, as such, and more about what might encourage human flourishing. So, very briefly, as popularly used, "ethics" is the study of individual and community morality – what individuals and the community think is "good" and "bad" – and the distillation, in a rational way, of that morality into ethical principles. In turn, ethical theory is the systematization of these ethical principles into an ethical framework or code, a pattern for living.

To move on from that, what might we, therefore, mean by the term "Christian ethics"? Well, in this sense it is a distillation of various principles informed (admittedly this is an Anglican/ Episcopalian formulation) by a combination of Scripture, tradition, and our God-given reason. And this collection, this system of ethics, has the purpose of allowing individuals and the community to determine how to act in an appropriate (or, to use a slightly more loaded word, "good") way in a range of different situations. So it is this system, this framework, of "Christian ethics" that we have first to articulate and then to internalize, thus allowing us to live our lives by it.

I am aware this already sounds terribly dry, so let's pull in some Scripture to try to help. What does Scripture tell us about "Christian ethics"? Well, there are at least two aspects.

The first are relatively clear commands, such as those in the Sermon on the Mount and the parable of the sheep and the goats. We are commanded to love our neighbour, and we are commanded to help the sick, the naked, the hungry, the prisoner, and all others who need our help. These are obviously crucial principles to live by, goals to aim for, but that's only part of it. An ethical code is not just about outcomes – important though they are – but also about how we get to those outcomes. So the second aspect revealed by Scripture is the importance of the means used for getting to them, as well as the good outcomes themselves.

To expand on this slightly, in ethical theory one of the big divides is between those theories focused on a good outcome, with less regard to the means of, or motives for, getting there; and between those theories that are less focused on the outcome than they are on the means, or on our motives in acting. Of course, the reality is that we need to focus on both. Outcomes are important, because we should aim to be effective rather than just right. But, equally, if we use whatever means we can to get to those outcomes then we may have damaged ourselves in the process. So, in addition to outcomes, both Jesus and Paul talk about the process of getting there, about motives. Think of what Jesus says about the Pharisees, who undoubtedly do the "right thing" but often for all the wrong reasons – hypocritically, to show off, to gain human praise. And, likewise, Paul talks about the importance of motives and means. Without faith and prayer we are nothing, he says. Without an acknowledgment of God we are nothing, whatever the outcomes may be.

But beyond the issue of whether one or the other (or both) is most important, is the question of how we integrate both a focus on means and a focus on ends into our everyday lives – integrate the two so that a search for ethical means and ethical ends becomes something natural, instinctive; subconscious, intuitive. In his book on ethics, Sam Wells (giving credit to Stanley Hauerwas) talks about this in terms of "ecclesial ethics". Through involvement in a church, or "ecclesial community", we learn the good habits. We internalize good practices – principles of Christian ethics – that allow us to live our lives in such a way that the right decisions will, hopefully, automatically be made. Why is this important? Well, most ethical theories tend to focus on the big decision – would it have been right to kill someone to stop them killing someone else? Can it ever be right to abort a foetus? Or, to come a little closer to home, would we resign from our job on this crucial point of principle? But, in fact, what ecclesial ethics demonstrates is that the big decision is often preceded by so many small ones that the outcome of the big decision is, effectively, preordained. We are the sum of our small decisions, and all of those will often make 99 per cent certain what our big decision will be. Our character is already set. To make sure we get the big decisions right, therefore, we need to make sure we get the small ones right. And to get those small ones right – most of which are done instinctively – we must have that framework already in place.

* * *

So, with this background, we come back to the question of how we react in the workplace when faced with an ethical dilemma. We may make the decision instinctively (the benefit of ecclesial ethics) and move on, but in other cases – particularly if it is a serious issue – we may have to stop and think. Our instinctive, but trained, reaction, even in small things, will be important for the example it may give to our fellow workers about how we live our lives. But it is in the larger decisions, ones where we may have consciously to pause and think and articulate our reasoning (even if our training essentially preordains the response), that the godly potential may be even more obvious. Because in that latter case, not only will we have made the right decision for ourselves and for the business (God's creation), but we may also have a much greater possibility of influencing our fellow workers for the future. So how do we go about this – this decision-making process and this articulation of our ethical beliefs in the workplace?

Well, and perhaps most importantly, we need to be very careful. If we quote Scripture at people, our influence is going to be close to zero. Some – many – businesses, particularly large ones, are institutionally allergic to religion of any flavour. And many of our fellow workers who don't share our faith will automatically assume that we are being judgmental if we appear to preach to them. So, despite the fact that we need to be very clear what our principles are, we also need some way to demonstrate that while we ourselves are guided by Christianity – both as to motives for what we do and as to achieving an appropriate outcome – there are also good non-faith reasons for following our course of action.

And that is where the passage from the Acts of the Apostles comes in. Paul arrives in Athens, which is still the intellectual centre of Greece, and, as usual, seeks to engage beyond the synagogue community with Gentiles. But in Athens he is dealing with significant thinkers, so instead of just laying out the gospel to them, he seeks to present it in their own language and using their own concepts – hence the "altar to the unknown god". Does he convince everyone? No. But is he given a hearing and allowed to get his message across? Yes. And that is what we should aim to do with ethics in the workplace: to use both our Christian background but also the everyday language of the workplace (for example, "respect", "fairness", and "diversity") to talk, when appropriate, about ethics. In that way we may have a measurable impact in a secularized environment while also being true to our principles and beliefs.

I want to come back to an idea that I mentioned earlier in this book and which I have found incredibly useful for explaining – to Christians and non-Christians alike – my attitude to ethics. (Or, put slightly differently, how I feel I can remain in a for-profit business while also being a priest.) This idea allows the bringing together of the insights of "ecclesial ethics" – focusing on getting the small decisions right through a pattern of daily behaviour – with a very practical focus on being an employee in the workplace. The American Franciscan, Richard Rohr, talks about a calling, a vocation, to live on the "edge of the inside". What he means by this is that you are not an angry voice standing outside the circle throwing rocks and insults at those inside – in our terms an angry, judgmental, Christian voice. But neither are you there in the centre, fully signed up defending everything that the "inside" stands for, ignoring your own code of Christian ethics simply because it's the inside.

To stand just inside the edge is to be on the inside as a worker – and to be recognized by your fellow workers as such – and it is to honour what the inside (here, the business) stands for. But to stand there is also to question the weaknesses and failings of the inside. This position allows us to ask the hard questions as workers – as employees of the business – in a language and from a position where we do not have to use overtly Christian terms. Hard questions, for example, about our own obligation to be honest. And hard questions of the business itself: how does it treat its employees and customers; how does it treat the local community around it; and how does it interact with, and add to, society as a whole?

Like Paul in Athens at the Areopagus, this allows us to show, to demonstrate, our distinctive Christian approach on ethics, but in language that stretches and expands people without threatening them with religion.

We always have to make decisions (tens, hundreds) every day in the workplace. Not all of them are ethical dilemmas, and some may not implicate Christian ethics – but some are, and some will. In the next nine chapters we will consider specific dilemmas that may arise in the workplace, such as being asked to lie or being tempted to do something bad. Many of these will be situations in which we have found ourselves over the years. But to return to the motif of the first section of this book, how might those events reveal – to us and to others – where Jacob's ladder is in the workplace? The answer is through our reactions to these workplace dilemmas and challenges. It's great when things are going well, but the true potential of the workplace, and the true potential we have as God's co-workers there, may only become obvious – perhaps may sometimes only be truly available – when something has gone wrong. When something has gone wrong, and we are called upon to act in front of our co-workers as sensitive, respectful, but totally authentic Christians who can make hard decisions well.

12

What Happens If... I am Asked to Do Something Against My Christian Beliefs?

1 Corinthians 10:25–33 (NRSV)

Eat whatever is sold in the meat market without raising any question on the ground of conscience, for "the earth and its fullness are the Lord's." If an unbeliever invites you to a meal and you are disposed to go, eat whatever is set before you without raising any question on the ground of conscience. But if someone says to you, "This has been offered in sacrifice," then do not eat it, out of consideration for the one who informed you, and for the sake of conscience – I mean the other's conscience, not your own. For why should my liberty be subject to the judgment of someone else's conscience? If I partake with thankfulness, why should I be denounced because of that for which I give thanks? So, whether you eat or drink, or whatever you do, do everything for the glory of God. Give no offence to Jews or to Greeks or to the church of God, just as I try to please everyone in everything I do, not seeking my own advantage, but that of many, so that they may be saved.

found much of my ordination training rather theoretical. To be sure, many things were useful to know, but not that many of them seemed of immediate practical application. One of the exceptions, however, was a session that we did on conflict resolution. The lecturer started off by drawing a big circle on a large sheet of paper, and then drawing a much smaller circle inside it. This large circle, she said, represents all of your beliefs and values. This much smaller circle represents your core beliefs, the things that make you who you are, and without which you would be someone different. That part of the larger circle that is outside the smaller one, however, represents your current views on things – but things about which you may not have thought too hard, or which change with the seasons. These things do not make you who you are in a fundamental sense, but more in a cocktail party-conversation sort of way. In a conflict situation, therefore, that outer part of the larger circle is what you can afford to give up to resolve that conflict without losing anything essential – anything that makes you "you". It is only the core that you have to hang on to. Not to overstate it, that's one of the most valuable lessons I have ever learned.

Just think about it for a moment. How often do we find ourselves arguing, fighting, over things that don't matter but over which we or our opponent have chosen to dig in our heels? A line in the sand; a matter of principle. But once we've taken that stand, the argument can't be resolved without someone backing down – without someone losing face. And so a cycle of conflict starts where, only too soon, people can't remember how it began or what the original argument was. And yet, because those positions have been taken, they become important of themselves. There will always be those who employ a military analogy and say that you need to defend your outer defences to weaken the enemy and protect the important inner defences. But is that appropriate in human interactions? Why create strife where it's unnecessary? "Blessed are the peacemakers," says Jesus in the Sermon on the Mount. And yet our culture – even our Christian culture – elevates a fight about principles over the need to make peace. Of course, often it's just another version of individualism. What *I* want or need is more important than the stability of the community in which I live. Here's what *I* think, and it's my right to think it. But even if we truly are talking about a core belief, do we ever really question whether we should be fighting for it, or whether a greater good might be served by stepping back?

I'll come back to this last question, because it's a crucial one, but first I want to look at the question of what might be core and non-core Christian beliefs. Presumably it's a core belief that Jesus is the Son of God who died that we might be forgiven? Well, yes, that sounds right. But how often in a workplace in the Western world are we going to be asked to deny that? Core is probably what's stated in the creeds, but even there, what about, for example, the virgin birth? Is that core? (Perhaps, but if Jesus was the Son of God – as I think we are required to believe – does it really matter exactly how He came to be on earth?) Core certainly does include the "Great Commandment" – love God, and love your neighbour as yourself. It probably covers the "Golden Rule" – do to others as you would have them do to you. But, again, it may well be that these never get challenged in your workplace, deeply secular though many workplaces may be.

What about wearing a cross at work? I understand I'm venturing onto dangerous ground here, and that some people take desperately seriously their ability to demonstrate their faith in this tangible way. But is it a core belief of Christianity? I don't think so. It doesn't appear in the Bible, and it's not necessarily really in the tradition of the church. So why have an argument about it? Even though it may be petty, and even spiteful, to forbid people to demonstrate their faith in the workplace in this way, is that worth fighting for? Does it advance the gospel to stand up for these "principles", or does it, perhaps, achieve the opposite? Does it speak of a defensive culture having recourse to the secular law to protect its position? Well, I've probably just given my answer. "Blessed are the peacemakers, for they will be called children of God" (Matthew 5:9 NRSV).

So, what core Christian principles might truly be put under strain in a twenty-first-century secularized workplace? Well, quite possibly those embodied in the parable of the sheep and the goats – helping the metaphorically starving, the thirsty, the stranger, the naked, the sick, and the prisoner. Helping the vulnerable and those who cannot look after themselves. But, in case that sounds too classically liberal, there are other "conservative" Christian principles that may also be put under strain in the workplace. For example, personal honesty and probity may constantly be tested. Or, perhaps, corrupt or monopolistic practices may place strain on the proper operation of the market and divert productive activity (the working with God that promotes the healing of creation) into something self-centred and possibly destructive. Wherever you stand on the spectrum, there are some big, core Christian principles that may come under challenge in the workplace.

What, then, are we to do about those principles? Well, let's turn to our Bible passage. In the Old Testament even fairly minor infractions of the Law could be the source of endless conflict: food laws, the Sabbath, intermarriage. (Take a look at Nehemiah.) But when we get to the New Testament something changes. Jesus, often and consistently, criticizes slavish adherence to the Law. But perhaps even more telling than Jesus' criticisms is the change undergone by Paul – the former

Pharisee, Saul. Despite being very definitely an argumentative figure, Paul was prepared to recede even on core issues. He had thrown physical circumcision away almost at the beginning of his ministry in order to get the Gentiles into the church. But the Council in Jerusalem had made clear that eating meat sacrificed to idols was the one food law they regarded as core. And yet, here we have Paul prepared to compromise in order to strengthen believers, and bring the word to others. Over a series of readings, of which this is only one, Paul says, look – the meat is created by God. So waving it in front of idols is not going to make it bad. But if the fact it has been sacrificed to idols is going to make some people waver in their belief, then you – the strong – even though you know it won't affect you, should not eat it, in order to help your fellows. Likewise, he says, if not eating meat is going to produce a big argument then that's not worth it either. In other words, do what is least likely to cause offence to others, and what is most likely to build up their faith.

Many principles, therefore, however important they may be, are rarely going to be worth a fight. But what if we are told to do something in the workplace that really, truly, definitively goes against the core of what Jesus taught? Well, again, I believe that "blessed are the peacemakers" is the best place to start. In another passage from the Sermon on the Mount, Jesus tells His listeners that if someone forces you to go one mile with them, then go the second – the extra mile – with them also. So, even if something is a core belief, we should go that extra mile to prevent it from becoming a conflict that will divide us. Even if it's something that annoys us, and even though the other person may be wrong, we are also told to forgive our brothers and sisters not seven times, but seventy times seven. Just in case you haven't got the message, Jesus keeps on repeating that fighting is not the way of God. It is giving ground to prevent conflict that is godly.

So, in order to preserve peace and harmony in the workplace we should try to find non-confrontational solutions. How? Isn't that easier said than done? Well, in fact, there are some very practical ways. We should first explore whether the person who appears to be crossing the line actually knows that they are doing so. Perhaps they don't understand the importance of what they are saying – the importance objectively or the importance to us. But if we go straight into attack-mode to set them right or to preserve our position, then we will provoke a response that will make their original intention quickly irrelevant – because once the fight has started it soon achieves a dynamic all of its own. And even if the person did truly intend to cross a line, by responding peacefully we may nevertheless be able to defuse the situation. By our being reasonable in the face of provocation the other person may be shamed into backing down – or even better, they may be positively impressed enough to back down. And perhaps they haven't fully thought through the implication of what they are saying. We'll consider this in more detail when we come to look at questions of cut-throat competition with our colleagues, or being asked to lie by our boss. But we should consider the possibility that it may be that the other person is under terrible pressure to achieve a certain result and so is flailing around looking for a solution. If we can find a way to help them, then we will have helped not just them but also ourselves.

But what if – after all of this – it does come to conflict and we are asked to do something which is clearly and unambiguously against our Christian beliefs? Well, the point that I have been seeking to make up until now is that I think those times actually come quite rarely. And that's not because I'm suggesting that people should compromise their beliefs or kid themselves that everything's great when it isn't, but more because I think the self-righteous adoption of positions, of judging, is something which as humans we should avoid at all costs. It is something that is often profoundly un-Christian. However, there may come that point when, in the workplace, we are invited to take up our cross and follow Jesus. That, for us, is not going to lead to a literal crucifixion. But if it involves the loss of a job, the disapproval of one's colleagues for rocking the boat, or difficulties at home because of the financial implications, then it's still going to be an intense physical experience.

But even if we are asked to do this thing against our core Christian beliefs and decide we cannot, how do we carry out that refusal? In going to the cross – the cross that He also tells us to take up – Jesus wasn't making a bloody-minded statement, He wasn't trying to bring about a fight, He wasn't seeking to intensify purifying violence. Exactly the opposite. He sacrificed Himself to start the process of breaking the cycle of violence by being the sacrifice of the person without any sin – to show the perversity and corruption of using violence to try to end violence. What Jesus tells us is that only non-violence can end violence. So even if we get to that point in the workplace where there is no alternative but to say "no" and take the consequences, we shouldn't use that as an opportunity to get up on our high horse and judge others; or as a reason to stir up our colleagues into some type of crusade; or as a reason to complain about anti-Christian persecution. We should make our case and state our reasons straightforwardly. We should do it without hesitation, but we should also do it without accusation. It is the way we act, and the manner of our departure, that will have the biggest influence on the future. If we shout and storm out, it may get a headline, it may change an HR process, but it won't trigger new thinking. If we walk away with our tail between our legs, that won't do any good either. But if we explain why we have to go – respectfully, but firmly, with integrity and with no desire to wound or hurt – that might (just might) make people think. That may crack open the old cycle of violence and conflict that feeds upon itself. And that is as true in the workplace as anywhere else.

We must, in the end, do what we believe is right – even at great cost to ourselves. And make no mistake (going back to the rather dismissive view some Christians have of paid work), losing a job, losing the approval of our fellow workers and our friends, losing a source of income, putting huge strains on our families – all of those are definitely "taking up our cross". But we must also be very careful about our motives. We need to be clear about whether something is a core principle or, rather, part of that wider, more transient group of views that we hold for the time being. We have to resist the temptation to take a stand or draw a line in the sand, if that is going to continue or exacerbate the cycle of conflict. Our responsibility as Christians is to end conflict, and we should be careful not to confuse that with being a noisy martyr. Very rarely will we be persecuted in the workplace for being a Christian. Much more often, when issues arise they come from an unintentional clash between Christian and secular principles. But if, in the end, we feel we must leave, we should go calmly, peacefully, even joyfully. If we whine or moan about it, or even worse if we sue to preserve our Christian "rights", we've completely missed the point. Our first duty in the workplace as a Christian is to avoid and lessen conflict – to bring the kingdom a step nearer. But if we do have to take up our cross, following Him who lived, and died, and rose for us, then we should celebrate, not complain.

13

What Happens If... I Am Told to Compete Against My Colleagues?

Matthew 25:14–28 (NRSV)

[Jesus said] "For it is as if a man, going on a journey, summoned his slaves and entrusted his property to them; to one he gave five talents, to another two, to another one, to each according to his ability. Then he went away. The one who had received the five talents went off at once and traded with them, and made five more talents. In the same way, the one who had the two talents made two more talents. But the one who had received the one talent went off and dug a hole in the ground and hid his master's money. After a long time the master of those slaves came and settled accounts with them. Then the one who had received the five talents came forward, bringing five more talents, saying, 'Master, you handed over to me five talents; see, I have made five more talents.' His master said to him, 'Well done, good and trustworthy slave; you have been trustworthy in a few things, I will put you in charge of many things; enter into the joy of your master.' And the one with the two talents also came forward, saying, 'Master, you handed over to me two talents; see, I have made two more talents.' His master said to him, 'Well done, good and trustworthy slave; you have been trustworthy in a few things, I will put you in charge of

*many things; enter into the joy of your master.' Then the one who
had received the one talent also came forward, saying, 'Master, I
knew that you were a harsh man, reaping where you did not sow,
and gathering where you did not scatter seed; so I was afraid, and
I went and hid your talent in the ground. Here you have what is
yours.' But his master replied, 'You wicked and lazy slave! You
knew, did you, that I reap where I did not sow, and gather where
I did not scatter? Then you ought to have invested my money with
the bankers, and on my return I would have received what was
my own with interest. So take the talent from him, and give it to
the one with the ten talents.'"*

Some of you may recall from earlier chapters that towards the beginning of my career I worked in a law firm which paid lip service to the idea of teamwork and collegiality but, in fact, promoted cut-throat competition through its compensation system. The system was known as "eat what you kill", and, while not literally true, it did lead to quite a lot of metaphorical blood flowing in the corridors. As I also said, it led in many ways to inefficiencies and under-utilization of other people's talents. What happened was that those partners who had the business hung on to it and sought to either exclude their fellow partners from that work or, alternatively, to neuter them so they posed no threat and became simply worker bees. It wasn't a great advertisement for competition, and the human costs were clear.

So, what should we do if we are told to compete with our fellow workers? Well, it won't surprise you to hear that my answer is "it depends". In the same way that stress can be destructive or constructive depending on the circumstances – driving us into utter despair or into new creativity – likewise competition can be beneficial or harmful. In the same way that the cut-throat law firm can be an unpleasant environment, so can the workplace where everyone is treated the same and rewarded in the same way regardless of the amount of effort they put in or initiative that they show. That can also deaden the spirit. So, it depends on the type of competition being called for and on the circumstances of the workplace. But, to put my cards on the table, I don't think that competition in the workplace is inherently un-Christian, despite the terrible results that it can sometimes lead to.

So, let's look first at some of the destructive forms of competition. In addition to my law firm example, another variant might be where people are told there is a limited pot of compensation, and any increase in their share in it can only come at the expense of their fellow workers. Of course, in all cases it will be true that the salary pot is limited in some way, but making that explicit can quickly poison the atmosphere. Once you know that you can only succeed at the expense of someone else, that will change the nature of your relationship with everyone else in the workplace. Your fellow worker will often go from being a friend, or someone with whom you cooperate, to someone who you try to one-up and with whom you have little incentive to cooperate.

And things can get even worse. Imagine that type of workplace where you were also told that, in addition to having to scramble over your colleagues to get more money, it will also be made public at the end of the year: who's up and who's down; who has succeeded and who has failed. So, to the lack of cooperation and suspicion of others, you add the possibilities of both humiliation and superiority, based on whether or not you managed to do your colleagues down. Research shows that organisations where everyone knows what everybody else earns are considerably less happy than those organisations where workers don't know that. And I know that's true. When my former boss called me up to discuss compensation, the one thing he invariably ended the conversation by saying was, "and, please, don't discuss this with anyone else".[3] And I always felt better. Even if I were the least jealous person in the world – which I am not – it would be hard not to feel a twinge of resentment over someone who gets more than you, even though you feel you do better/try harder/work longer than they do. And, equally, I can easily envisage others resentfully thinking that they were being severely undercompensated vis-à-vis me. So, this type of public, recognized competition can poison the workplace, poison the human relationships, and deaden its godly potential.

How about one final scenario? You're a department of twenty people and you're told that five people will have to be sacked from the department in a year's time, so it's up to you to show that you're better than at least five others over the next twelve months. What can you do? You need that job. You know that others also need that job. You know they'll stop at nothing. So you feel you'd better stop at nothing – and that you need to be better at stopping-at-nothingness than the others. You try to imagine what they might do; and then do it quicker, harder, dirtier than they do. For good relationships between human beings and, ironically, often for the good of the business, it's a recipe for disaster. And, sadly, it's not nearly as rare as it should be.

Being asked to compete against our fellow workers can be bad for us in terms of what it does to us and our relations with others, bad for those other people, and bad for the business and God's purpose for it – its place in creation – if in fact it is destroying relationships and potential, rather than creating them. Competition can be destructive.

So, what does the Bible have to say about competition?

---

3   I should make very clear that this was not a rule, or a condition of the new compensation – it was a simple request. There are occasions where workers are being exploited, and being forbidden from sharing salary and benefit information would then diminish the potential of the workplace rather than enhancing it.

Well, in this area, people with very different points of view can fish around for lots of texts to support them. There are those who think that competition is bad and point to parables, such as the one about the labourers in the vineyard who turned up at different times but all got paid the same. Or to Jesus denouncing the Pharisees, who with their public piety compete for public approval. Or to Jesus telling James and John not to argue over who is the greatest, but to engage in radical new thinking where those who want to be first must be the servants of all, and the last shall be first. Or to some of the stories in the Acts of the Apostles about how the early church held property in common and did everything for the good of the community. And then there's the idea of justification by faith – the idea that Christ freed us from our sins by dying for us – and the understanding that the gift of this saving grace is open to us regardless of anything that we ourselves do. That also seems to negate competition to make God love us more than others. If we accept God's love, He will love us – and will love as many of us as love Him without any numerical limit.

But the believers in tooth-and-claw competition aren't short of texts either. They can point to many Old Testament stories where the Jewish people were in constant competition with their neighbours, and – as the subject was often land – by definition could only succeed at the expense of the other peoples. There are also many Old Testament characters in competition with one another who seem to be approved of, starting with the patriarchs, including Abraham and Jacob. In the New Testament, Paul often uses sporting analogies talking about people preparing for a race, and about there being only one winner. And then, of course, there's the parable of the talents, which we have read above (and one to which we will also return in much greater detail in the final section).

This is a story that provokes strong reactions. To some it

seems an indefensible promotion of the idea of inequality. Those who have much get more; those who have less have even that taken away. Additionally, the harsh master is not condemned. Far from it: what he does seems to become the point, the "moral" almost, of the story. This seems the classic story of capitalism. A parable that does not deserve to be in the Bible. For supporters of competition (and inequality, perhaps) it seems the perfect parable. The successful are rewarded because in a competitive marketplace they've worked hard, taken what their master has given them and made something of it. They've used their opportunity, their resources, their talents, and they have created wealth by their active involvement (the unsuccessful slave is criticized for not even putting the money in the bank to earn a little interest).

So, case closed? Successful competition is rewarded, and failure is punished? Well, I'm not sure it's actually quite that cut and dried. First, of course, this is a parable, not a literal endorsement of the facts of the story. But, more importantly, this is not actually about competition of the type that we have been discussing. The slaves are not set up in opposition to each other. This is not some first-century version of *The Apprentice*. Rather, they are each given something to look after on their own. There is no indication that when the talents are first handed out they were told that the successful one would be further rewarded, or that the least successful would be penalized. In fact, they are each operating independently. For each of them, the competition is against himself, or against the system. It is a call to individual effort and achievement, rather than destructive competition. Nor is it an endorsement for inequality resulting from competition. It is only because the one talent slave has not used that talent that it gets taken away from him – not because he was last. The moral of the story – at least for me – is that we must make the best of what we have, whatever that may be, rather than that the winner takes it all.

A helpful analogy for me here is that of academic exams. I have always disliked face-to-face competition because that implies a winner and a loser. (Maybe it's just because I'm lousy at sports, but I think it goes broader than that.) By contrast, I've always liked exams. I know that certain grades are limited, but it's not competition against another person. It's more competition against the system. In a given year if more people are exceptional, then more people will do well. That's the parable of the talents for me. Doing the best with what you've got – but not as a zero-sum game with your colleagues.

The possibilities of this in the workplace seem pretty clear. If we're not competing against each other, but rather striving to be the best we can be, then competition might become a positive thing. The one talent slave is condemned for his passivity, not because he was last. So we can strive to be the best we can be without clambering over others and doing them down. Passivity can be a bad thing. In earlier chapters we looked at the theologian Miroslav Volf, and at his idea that we all have a positive part in God's work of creation – in the building up, the healing, of that which will be made perfect at the end of time. But if we just sit around moping, or feeling sorry for ourselves, or doing the bare minimum as we count the days until retirement, then we are not participating as fully in that work of creation as we could do.

I don't want to paint too rosy a picture of my own workplace, but I believe it does contain many of these elements of positive competition. (In fact, I wouldn't be there if it had that destructive form.) I am surrounded by bright, driven, A-type personalities – often a recipe for disaster – but partly because of the structure of the organization, and partly because of the characters involved, the atmosphere is not personally competitive. Partly, it's because my boss has around twenty direct reports and we're all pretty much at the same level, so we're not jockeying position among ourselves – or for her job. Partly, it's because we all trust each other not to try to do the other down. And, partly, it's because we understand very clearly that our individual efforts feed into the collective effort, and if the collective effort is successful then so will we all be individually.

In today's political environment, I'm going to be cautious about claiming too much for the benefits of cooperative competition in a large multinational corporate tax department, but there are other parts of our business where it also works very well. In our research division, for example, people cooperate in teams to build better products – smaller medical devices, more fuel-efficient jet engines. And there can even be rare examples in the workplace where direct competition against others (as opposed to the faceless "competition") may be beneficial. If sales teams compete to sell a good product – and they are incentivized by reward – then what they learn about the best way to sell can be passed on to other teams in order to improve the performance of all teams. Of course, this has to be handled carefully, so that it doesn't turn into destructive competition, but there is, at least, the potentiality for something creative.

So, what do you do if you are asked to compete in the workplace? Well, the first question is what type of competition? If it involves direct personal competition with your colleagues where there have to be winners and losers, then you should be very, very careful. There are some absolutely central teachings of Jesus on the matter, and the potential damage to you is also very real. On the other hand, if it is competition against the system, or striving to be the best you can be, then the message from the parable of the talents may be that that is entirely appropriate – or even, in fact, what God wants. So we must certainly be very careful, but not all competition in the workplace is bad. In fact, a lack of ambition, satisfaction with the mediocre, living in a monochrome world, is maybe not what God wants either. And, occasionally, competition may be what it takes to stir it up, to return some intensity to the colours, to get closer to what God intends for us.

14

What Happens If... My Boss Wants Me to Work Harder and Harder?

Psalm 127:1-2 (NRSV)

Unless the Lord builds the house,
those who build it labour in vain.
Unless the Lord guards the city,
the guard keeps watch in vain.
It is in vain that you rise up early
and go late to rest,
eating the bread of anxious toil;
for he gives sleep to his beloved.

There's an old preacher's story about a newly minted management consultant who takes a rare day off from the big city to go to the coast. It might be somewhere on the Mediterranean; it might be somewhere on the Pacific. Our man positions himself at a bar in the harbour fairly early in the morning and watches the world go by. When he first arrives he sees a fisherman go out in his small boat. The fisherman returns two hours later with an absolutely beautiful tuna, the finest fish our consultant has ever seen. But the fisherman immediately sells it for a pittance to a fish broker right on the quayside. The fisherman then has a three-hour lunch with his family, then a three-hour siesta, then three hours of drinking and playing cards with his friends, and then the family evening meal. Well, our management consultant can't stand the inefficiency. So he asks to talk to the fisherman. He explains how, if he fished for longer, then he could afford to hire another fisherman. This would increase his profit, and with the increased money, he could then buy more boats. With more boats, and more people working for him, his profits would increase further. With the increased money from that he could cut out the middleman, stop fishing himself, and go to the big city to sell the fish. Once there, he could raise money on the stock market, buy a canning factory, diversify out of tuna. Then he could go international. "But why would I do this?" the fisherman asks. "Why all of that work, living in the big city, spending time away from my family?" Our management consultant smiles as he delivers what he knows is the winning argument. "The ultimate aim," he says, "is to put yourself in the position where a larger company will buy you out. With all the money that you've earned, you can retire, buy a house by the sea, go fishing for a few hours in the morning, eat lunch with your family, sleep in the afternoon, and socialize with friends in the evening."

Well, you get the picture. It's become commonplace, a cliché really, that as a society each of us has to work harder, faster, all the time. For those of us that feel that way, we use any number of reasons – or excuses – to justify this: the difficult economic situation; the universal reach of electronic devices that keep us connected to work when not at our desks; global competition that means that there's someone out there (usually abroad) prepared to do our job for a fraction of the price – so we'd better work harder or else. This can be overstated. There probably never was a golden age when everyone worked nine to five, could read to their children every night, and had all their weekends free. And it's also true, as we've discussed a little before, that many people don't have jobs at all, or are in jobs that they loathe so much that they'd never put in an extra minute. But while the perception may be more extensive than the truth, there is, nevertheless, also some reality there. The economic situation in many Western countries means that we really do need to hang on to our jobs because it may be difficult to get another. Globalization really does pose challenges to certain industries and sectors in which labour costs are one of the biggest elements in the price of the goods or services. And iPhones and BlackBerries do connect us to the workplace the whole time.

So what exactly is the nature of the dilemma for those who are forced (or feel some pressure to force themselves) to work harder? I think to understand that, and to move on to the question of how we should react, we need to focus on four relationships that may be affected by working harder and harder. First, our relationship with our family. Second, that with ourselves. Third, that with our work itself. And, fourth, that with God.

Let's start with the family. I think we probably all smile when we read one of those summer news stories about the frustrated spouse on holiday who, after days of being ignored, eventually rips the BlackBerry/iPhone out of his or her spouse's hand and tosses it into the swimming pool. "Hooray!" we all think, as we instinctively, nervously, pat our side to make sure that our own phone is still there. But there's a fundamental point. Relationships, particularly those we have agreed to be seriously committed to, take real, undivided attention – and sometimes quite a lot of undivided attention. I'm actually a fan of my iPhone, because I know it enables me to be somewhere other than physically in the office, when previously that would not have been possible. But I also know that however good I think I am at multi-tasking, in reality if I am trying to do one thing, I will not give the other my full attention. And quite often you can't do human relationships in twenty-minute blocks. It may work for speed-dating, but spouses, kids, and close friends need more than that. They need in some way to know that they are important to you; and snuggling up to them while you continue to write emails doesn't quite do it. You may think they don't notice, and you're doing pretty well. But all of sudden it will emerge that, actually, you've been downgrading the relationship over a long period of time, and upgrading it again will be very difficult. Time not spent on relationships, especially with children, may not come round again. And believe me, I speak from experience. So, while we were put on earth to help God as His co-workers in the world, we were also put here to be in relationship with other people to help them and grow with them. The healing of creation is not just about making things; it's even more about people, relationships.

The second relationship is the one we have with ourselves. Many people are never going to have the time to spend hours each day in prayer and contemplation. But, in order to be able to make sense of our life, we need occasionally to step back from it and take a good hard look. I know, again from my own experience, that the first thing that goes when I get busy is the quiet time. Hurried prayers on the run, cramming a Bible reading into the last minutes of wakefulness are just about better than nothing. But they don't bring any of the real benefits of contemplation, of filtering the events of our day, our lives, in order to discover true priorities. Hard work can be interesting, it can be rewarding, and quite often it can even be fun. But it doesn't refresh the soul. It doesn't provide perspective. It quite simply provides no time for us to ask important questions of ourselves. So we barrel forward at great speed. We may earn enormous financial rewards. We may be highly praised. But we will never know – at least not until it is far too late – the roads not taken, the opportunities, the possibilities for development passed by. We may, quite simply, have in some way missed the opportunity to be fully human.

The third relationship I mentioned was with work itself. There's a very obvious point, which nevertheless needs to be made, and that's about burnout. If we are no longer capable of doing the job, then we will have done to the work, our colleagues, our customers, a disservice just as great as the one we have done ourselves. But there's also a subtler point. Almost all work requires some creativity. To be sure, any ideas need carrying through into practice, into action; otherwise they'll just be ideas. But if all we're doing is rushing at such speed that we never pause to think about what it is that we're really doing, or what's wrong with it, or how it could be done better, then we may not do it very well at all. Again, I think you may recognize that in yourselves from time to time.

Now this area is an example of where some of the theological ideas that we have previously looked at can help provide perspective. I talked about Miroslav Volf and his idea that with the Holy Spirit we are co-workers in building up, in healing God's creation. For that to be effective, however, it requires us to stop and think, to try to discern where the Spirit may actually be leading us. It also requires us to stop and think about whether we are contributing to the healing of God's creation – or, perhaps, harming it. All of that takes time, and if we're working so hard that all we can focus on is getting through the next day, or next week, or next month, it's unlikely we'll ask ourselves the questions. The Holy Spirit will still be there – but if we're not listening He might as well not be. So, burnout and lack of creativity are actually bad for the job itself and will be made worse, not better, by working ever harder.

The final relationship we need to look at is that with God. In a sense the three preceding relationships all touch also on this fourth relationship – time with our family and friends, time for contemplation, and being co-workers in creation. God is present, centrally present, in all of those. But there is one additional thing. The harder we work, the more – quite often – we come to believe that whatever we do, whatever we achieve, we do by our own human efforts, by our own merits. That's wrong – although, to be clear, God won't be offended and strike you down. However, it does mean that when we need God, for example when the job fails or when something catastrophic happens to the family, then, in fact, not just one but three things can go wrong. First, there is the disaster itself. Second, and at the same time, our illusion of self-sufficiency is also shattered, making it even harder to cope. Third, on top of all that, if we've been ignoring God in our mad onward rush, then we may have absolutely no idea how to find Him precisely when we realize we need Him. So we are hit not once, but three times, by the same event.

It is to this that our very short Bible passage goes – although it is of a piece with others (about, for example, not being able to add an inch to our height by worrying) that show the error and, in many cases, the futility, of thinking that we can rely solely on ourselves and are in control of everything. We can do great things with God, but we need to be very clear that it is with God, not on our own. And work, hard work, work that may affect the very way our brain works, blinds us to that fact.

So, eventually, to the question in hand. What do we do if our boss just keeps piling on the pressure to work harder and harder? I'm not sure, as usual, that there's a simple answer. To start off, we do have to be objective. Are we simply being asked to do what our job requires when we would like to do less? There are benefits to work and to stretching ourselves to reach a level of creativity using our gifts in cooperation with the Holy Spirit. So we need to be a little careful. But let's assume that's not the case, that things are getting out of hand, and all four of those relationships are suffering. Again, as you'll have gathered by now, confrontation is not my preferred approach. So we first need to ask whether we're doing it to ourselves – I'm certainly guilty of that. It may make it easier at home if I tell them that the company, my boss, is making me do it. But if I'm doing it to myself, and it's creating a problem, then some real honesty is crucial.

To carry on, however, if it really is your boss – let's assume now that he's trying to squeeze even more productivity out of his "assets" – then perhaps you talk to your fellow workers to see if it's a common perception. Perhaps you talk to your boss directly. If that's too scary, go talk to HR. But, some of you will say, that will be a black mark on my record. I still think that if you put your case reasonably – if you explain the family circumstances, or why you think it's making you do your job less well – you should get a fair hearing. But if you don't, that also tells you something. As I just said, we shouldn't be confrontational, but I believe equally strongly that if something is a problem, then (as with an attack on core Christian principles) doing nothing simply isn't an option. But you might say back, I need the job, my family needs it, and I'll never get anything like it elsewhere.

Well, there are two points to make here. The first, as we discussed when looking at the P45/pink slip, is that you don't know that. Think back to the story of Moses and the Israelites leaving Egypt and apply it to your workplace. Leaving a place where Pharaoh and his Egyptians have you toiling over their pyramids in return for a subsistence wage may open up new and better opportunities. But those perspectives will only emerge once you've jumped off the treadmill. Yes, you may find yourself, like the Israelites, in the desert, the wilderness, for a while, but that will not last forever. And second, if the job is bad for you in all the ways that we've just described because you have to work harder and harder, then you owe it to each of those four relationships to give it up.

I have a good friend whose husband recently lost his job. Their life had become incredibly complicated because of the amount they both worked. When the axe fell, it looked like a disaster. Six months later it was clear it was the opposite. That's not to say it was all easy or that they didn't worry about money. But the family as a whole was healthier and happier; the relationships were stronger – and that's because someone could provide the time to pull it all together.

We shouldn't sugar-coat the past, but if we do feel that we are being asked to work harder and harder then we have to do something about it; otherwise relationships will be damaged. To go back to the old fisherman in the story I told at the beginning, he understood the truth of this in a way that the management consultant did not – perhaps could not. He did work hard to get his tuna, although he sold it for a modest sum. He already valued time with his family and friends. He had time for contemplation. And I'm guessing he acknowledged that what he had came from something other than simply his own human endeavours (from the fruitfulness of God). In the end the greatest danger of too much work is that it persuades us that our own human endeavour and striving is the only thing that matters. It isn't, and we should try to remove anything that convinces us that it is. "It is in vain that you rise up early and go late to rest, eating the bread of anxious toil: for he gives sleep to his beloved."

15

What Happens If... Someone Has to Take the Blame?

John 15:9–14 (NRSV)

[Jesus said] "As the Father has loved me, so I have loved you; abide in my love. If you keep my commandments, you will abide in my love, just as I have kept my Father's commandments and abide in his love. I have said these things to you so that my joy may be in you, and that your joy may be complete. This is my commandment, that you love one another as I have loved you. No one has greater love than this, to lay down one's life for one's friends. You are my friends if you do what I command you."

Some of you may have read William Golding's *Lord of the Flies* about a group of British boarding schoolboys marooned on a tropical island and their descent into barbarism. If you have, you may remember that at those types of schools there coexists both a detailed and formalized code of schoolboy honour, and a very primitive but strong kill-or-be-killed survival instinct. Early in my first year at boarding school I decided that I should take the blame for something that I hadn't done. If I didn't take the blame, it would fall on another boy who also wasn't at fault, but was (I decided) less able to look after himself. So, true to that code of honour, I summoned up my courage and went down to my Housemaster's study and took the blame. I think it was such a novelty for him to have this happen that he decided not to punish me. Heartened by this, I went back to my dormitory (the communal bedroom shared with ten other boys) and told what I thought was this encouraging tale. Soon, however, my Housemaster heard that I'd talked about it, assumed I'd been boasting about how I'd tricked him, and spent the rest of his tenure making my life difficult. As this stage unfolded, the second (kill-or-be-killed) instinct kicked in: note to file – no good ever comes of owning up to anything.

As it turns out, that also appears to have been the lesson learned by the larger world. It seems that hardly anyone in "authority" is prepared to take the blame for something that they did, far less something that someone else did. The classic formulation of public acceptance of blame over the last twenty years has been what we might call the "Clintonian passive". The Clinton Administration (and those since) was famous for frequent admissions that "mistakes were made". That's good, you might say – until you realize that the active tense, with the implication of personal responsibility, is: "I made a mistake." And that's rather different from saying "mistakes were made".

So, let's talk about this in relation to the workplace and look a little more closely at "taking the blame". The answer to the threshold question of why taking the blame might be important, at least in one sense, seems quite simple. It's because something has gone wrong, something caused by human error – or intentional act – that in some way causes harm to others. Put differently, someone gets hurt. So, if someone is hurt, then obviously, we might say, someone should apologize – but is that the same as taking the blame? An apology ("I am sorry") will undoubtedly help individual healing, not least in the realization for the victim that it was not their fault, that they need not feel guilt. But beyond this, what does someone taking the blame ("It was my fault") actually achieve?

Well, I think that if apologizing is about people, about healing them, then taking the blame is more systemic. It is about putting the business ecosystem, the community that is the business, right again. It is about healing that body. Now, of course, there are dangers in the word "blame". It is possible that a requirement to take the blame – as opposed to an apology – might actually feed an unhealthy thirst for vengeance and suggest a return to an older retributional ethic of an eye for an eye. I would argue that while it should definitely not be about vengeance, "taking the blame" is nevertheless important for the benefits it brings to the entire community of the workplace. Before getting further into that, however, let's look at some situations in the workplace and ask whether "taking the blame" might be a step on the road to healing.

These items can range from macro, affecting the whole workplace, to micro, affecting only a single person. In that first category consider the following:

- Perhaps the CEO decides to undertake a massive reorganization, or a substantial acquisition, as a vanity project. It may be that the reorganization upsets the dynamics inside the company but produces no compensating economic benefits. Or perhaps the difficulties of integrating the acquired company have not been thought through. Or the price paid is too high, so "fat" (i.e. human beings) has to be cut to bring margins back to profitable levels. **Net result:** a less successful, less happy, and less productive company – where, more often than not, the "failed" CEO then departs with an attractive golden handshake.

- Perhaps the senior management push past the quiescent shareholders a very rich executive compensation scheme that widens inequality inside the firm, but which leads to no discernible increases in productivity, return on investment, or any other economic measure. **Net result**: overpaid execs and much disgruntlement below that.

- Perhaps senior management encourage short-termism and increased risk-taking in order to boost quarterly or annual results (for the knock-on effect on salary, stock options, and bonuses) with no regard to the long-term risk that is accumulated. **Net result**: increasingly aggressive behaviour and long-term pain for most of the regular employees (and for the shareholders – and, sometimes, for the taxpayers).

In each case, the health of the workplace, the business as a whole, has been damaged by ill thought through or selfish acts by a handful of individuals. As my CEO put it: "I think we are at the end of a difficult generation of business leadership, and maybe leadership in general. Tough-mindedness, a good trait – was replaced by meanness and greed – both terrible traits. Rewards became perverted. The richest people made the most mistakes with the least accountability."[4] That's a lot of hurt to people, and to businesses; that's a lot of healing that needs to happen.

And at the micro end, there are many of the things we have mentioned in other chapters:

- Perhaps there is an ineffective junior manager who cannot keep his small team in order, with the result that warfare breaks out. **Net result**: the entire team is less productive and totally unhappy.

---

4   Immelt, J., "Renewing American Leadership", Speech at US Military Academy, West Point, 9 December 2009, http://files.gereports.com/wp-content/uploads/2009/12/90304-2-JRI-Speech-Reprint1-557.qxd_8.5x11.pdf.

- Perhaps there is one employee who, in their dislike of a fellow employee, spreads vicious and untrue rumours about that employee to other employees. **Net result**: the gossiper, the gossiped-about, and the listener are all diminished.

- Perhaps one employee, with crass insensitivity towards the personal difficulties of another employee, keeps trespassing on a personal issue. Or perhaps naked ambition leads us to elbow a colleague aside in our desire for promotion or more money. Or perhaps we mess up and then try to cover up by trying to convince others that it was somebody else's fault. **Net result in all of these cases**: a less happy and less productive workplace, and hurt inflicted upon individuals.

What unites all of these, whether macro or micro, is that the workplace will be diminished. And, as we've said before, that damages the potential for the healing of God's creation that should be happening in the workplace.

So let's come back to the question of whether "taking the blame", including in the workplace, is actually a good thing to do. I think it is, but perhaps not in quite as simple a way as the question might indicate. In the last chapter of this section ("What Happens If... I Do Something Bad in the Workplace?"), we'll look at the personal benefits to each of us of taking the responsibility when we've done something wrong. But here I'd like to talk about the systemic benefits of someone taking the blame, the benefits to the communal body as a whole, to the entire workplace – the possibility of healing for a workplace community if someone is prepared to go beyond "I am sorry" to "I personally take the blame".

So, what might those communal benefits be of one person bearing the blame? Well, let's turn to John's Gospel. The New Testament presents us with two starkly competing models. In this chapter's Bible passage we have Jesus' words during the

Last Supper about there being no greater love than laying down one's life for one's friends, for one's community. As I'll explain, that is one way of "taking the blame". But there is the alternative view in the ambiguous statement of Caiaphas, the Chief Priest, that it would be better for one – innocent – man to die for the people, rather than the whole nation perish. One talks about love; the other seems a cynical sacrifice of an innocent. But both focus on the issue of "taking the blame", and on what is best for the community.

Let's look at Caiaphas first. Steeped in the tradition of the Torah, he may well have been thinking of the various types of offerings specified in Mosaic Law and, in particular, sin offerings. These were effective (but never more than temporary) palliatives against godly anger and/or human failings. So, in Leviticus 16, for example, two goats are to be brought to the priest as a sin offering. One is sacrificed, but the other has all the sins of Israel "confessed upon its head", is then taken out in the wilderness a long way from the camp, and is set free to roam, carrying the people's sins with it. What did Caiaphas have in mind when he referred to Jesus' death? We don't know. But some type of offering, sacrifice, propitiation – perhaps not so much to God as to the occupying powers – may have been in his mind. And, perhaps, also a sacrifice to keep his own people united in the face of Jesus' challenge. Sin offering or scapegoat, Jesus becomes the means this week, this month, this year, of buying off trouble from an angry God, or angry enemies, or his own angry community. So Caiaphas looks to pin the blame on someone else to propitiate, to pacify – for however short a time – God, the people, or blind fate.

But what is Jesus talking about? How does it differ? What does He mean about taking the blame by laying down one's life? Another blood sacrifice, another propitiation? Absolutely not. Drawing on a different Old Testament tradition, Jesus is talking about sacrificial love – an innocent taking on blame to promote healing, not to buy off trouble; an innocent taking on blame to allow new growth, rather than stasis and fruitless circularity. Jesus may well be pointing out the weaknesses of the old sacrificial system. But, it seems to me, there is also something incredibly positive here. In order to change things – to really change things – someone has to show the depth of their love for others. Someone has to show an understanding that to bring healing in the community, to make the next day better than the last, an example (often at personal cost) has to be set. That's not a sacrifice to placate anger; that's a sacrifice to set an example which may make people think differently the next time.

But, we might ask, can we all be Maximilian Kolbe, for example, taking the blame after a death camp escape, voluntarily swapping places at Auschwitz so that another person (a husband and father) might live? Probably not, certainly speaking personally. But is there the possibility that his example, and that of others, might make us think harder in a lesser situation, say in the workplace, about what might promote healing? Yes. About what might make the business a better place where the work of creation can flourish? Yes. About what might make the business a better citizen where it can contribute to the community around it? Yes. And, in each case, will that mean keeping quiet or speaking up?

If something has gone wrong, I need to ask what might be the benefit to the community of me saying that – even if I am not completely at fault – "I personally take the blame." What benefit might accrue to the community if I sacrifice my pride, my bonus, my mask of self-esteem, my carefully constructed public reputation, my status, even my job? It would be painful, yes, but that is not a sin offering, a blood offering. It is, instead, the start of healing.

Let's look at a real workplace example (at the macro end of the scale). In 2011 the then-CEO of Barclay's Bank, Bob Diamond, famously said – after pretty much nobody had taken the blame for the financial crisis – that the time for "remorse" was over. Well, perhaps – if "remorse" means hand-wringing and navel gazing. But the time for taking the blame had not passed (nor has it now). To be very clear, this is not about "taking the blame" so that bankers can be punished, and not so that the public can relish a modern-day sin sacrifice (or exiled scapegoat). It is about taking the blame for the sake of the community of the workplace, for the business system. Taking the blame so that the process of healing can start, inspired by the example of leaders admitting they themselves made a mistake (no passive voice there), that the hurt they caused and the damage done had a human cause (not fate), that the hurt affected other human beings, and that the next generation of leaders must act differently, think differently. If that were to happen, no one needs to be sacrificially slaughtered on an altar. But if that were to happen, the trust of people in their leaders, in the business, in their fellow workers could begin to heal and then to grow; and the work of healing God's creation in the community that is the business could start afresh. And, of course, this is equally true on the micro level, for the bad manager of a small team, the office gossip, the ambitious office climber. If they take the blame, then the communal healing can start. That is the message of Jesus in laying down His life for His friends. That is the message of the resurrection.

So, to return to *Lord of the Flies*: civilization is only skin deep, and as human beings we are a mass of contradictory and competing impulses. But sacrificial love, "taking the blame", whether large or small can be a sign of God in the world – not a sign of our own goodness, or our own bravery, but of what, with God, we can achieve. And that type of example may, just may, inspire others to also seek out what God may be looking for the next time hurt has been caused, and healing needs to occur. Very few of us (strange schoolboys aside) will often, if ever, take the blame for something that someone else has done. But we can all – should all – take the blame for what we have done. Not just for the good of our eternal souls, but for the good of the community. This is important in our everyday lives, in our workplaces – not just the big life-and-death decisions. If we can be encouraged to do this, then we may be able to move to a better place where healing occurs, where trust is restored, and where fruitful cooperation with God in His ongoing process of creation in the workplace can begin again.

16

What Happens If...
Everyone's Always
Arguing?

Matthew 22:15–22 (NRSV)

Then the Pharisees went and plotted to entrap him in what he said. So they sent their disciples to him, along with the Herodians, saying, "Teacher, we know that you are sincere, and teach the way of God in accordance with truth, and show deference to no one; for you do not regard people with partiality. Tell us, then, what you think. Is it lawful to pay taxes to the emperor, or not?" But Jesus, aware of their malice, said, "Why are you putting me to the test, you hypocrites? Show me the coin used for the tax." And they brought him a denarius. Then he said to them, "Whose head is this, and whose title?" They answered, "The emperor's." Then he said to them, "Give therefore to the emperor the things that are the emperor's, and to God the things that are God's." When they heard this, they were amazed; and they left him and went away.

Some people just love a good argument. Nothing seems too small to argue over. Nothing too insignificant to let go. When I was at college I had a friend who would greet almost every statement I made with the question: "Why?" (I, as you will have gathered, do not terribly like arguing.) "But why?" she would say, and I knew I faced two alternatives: argue over the basics or give in. It could be a little exhausting. However, I was back at my old university a few months ago, and talking to one of the professors about the difficulty a new (adult) arrival was having with the relentlessly questioning atmosphere among the academics there. "But they have to understand," he said, "that's how we do our work. It's only out of hard arguments that genuinely new answers emerge." And he was right, of course. Consensual thinking is often going nowhere. It's comfortable, it's secure, but it's also stasis. It is often only out of rigorous examination, the clash of ideas, the operation of the dialectic, frequently involving other people whose views are very different to our own, that something new, valuable, and creative can emerge.

So what's the answer? Should some people argue less, or should those of us who find it too hot in the (argumentative) kitchen get out of there? Well, to switch this from a college to a workplace, let's for a moment consider the types of arguments that can take place, some of which can be positive, even energy-giving, and others which are, at best, distracting, and sometimes actually destructive. I want to consider three basic types: constructive, destructive, and righteous (which can combine elements of the first two in various measures).

Let's start with constructive arguments. Sometimes my colleagues are faced with significant technical tax problems – which I hasten to add may not be totally disreputable, but rather relate to the complexity of the interaction of various different provisions of tax law and our business's own very complicated facts. While they can be painful, there's no doubt that sometimes large meetings where everyone stays in the room arguing the technicalities until the problem is solved can be productive. Some people may come away feeling bruised if their pet theory gets trampled on, but the overall result is likely to be better. And by extension, I know that my own policy thinking is likely to be improved if exposed to the arguments of my colleagues. I may occasionally hope that I have thought of every angle, every pro and con, but I can guarantee you that I haven't. Again, it may be a bit bruising – for me this time – but I'll have a better product, a better set of policy arguments that I can make in the end.

Now, of course, a lot depends on how this type of argument is conducted. If the people are taking real pleasure in destroying someone else's argument, in viciously ripping it apart, then it will obviously be considerably less energy-giving than if it is done without a desire to in some way destroy the other. But done constructively, if we're seeking to improve something, this type of argument will often be positive, whether we're talking about the performance of an aircraft engine, a medical scanner, a sales team, or a legal argument. And, respectfully done, the more rigorous the questioning, the better the final product will be.

But that's only one type of arguing. What about the second, entirely negative type? There are, as we've already mentioned, those people who just love picking a fight. It doesn't have to be, often probably won't be, about work itself. But the negative feelings that it engenders can certainly poison the entire atmosphere in the workplace. It may be about money, it may be about the workplace rules, it may be over a perception of favouritism, it may be over football teams. Who knows? But if there is constant bickering so that everything has an edge, then, as we have noted before, the potential for the workplace to be a place where we can all participate fruitfully in the healing of creation will be damaged.

So what are we to do? Well, let's turn to the Bible. Two short passages almost immediately jump out at us. From the beatitudes in Matthew's Gospel, Jesus tells us, "Blessed are the peacemakers" (5:9). That seems pretty straightforward. And another one perhaps: "If anyone strikes you on the right cheek, turn the other also" (5:39). So we have a clear obligation to make peace, and we have an obligation not to rise to an argument. Case closed? Well, perhaps not. For people like me there is the distinctly uncomfortable fact that the Jesus of the Gospels – the Son of God – is actually pretty argumentative. He was forever arguing with the Pharisees, to the extent that fairly early on in His ministry they began to look for ways to get rid of Him. He argued with the lawyers, calling them a brood of vipers. He accused them of building tombs for the dead prophets but killing the living ones. He was also skilled in dealing with arguments that others started. He often, for example, parried the question of whether He claimed to be the Son of God and, perhaps most famously, turned the argument back on the questioner when asked whether it was lawful to pay taxes to Caesar (our Bible passage above). Jesus spent a lot of time arguing. But what was important for Him was arguing over things that mattered, and not over everything. We're going to look more at anger in the next chapter, but Jesus was, of course, profoundly aware of the destructive nature of anger. He was also aware of the dangers of injustice, of false teaching, of replacing heavenly values with human ones. And those were things worth arguing over.

So where does that leave us? Well, I think where argument has positive potential, that's a balancing act. If in the end it is going to lead to a better product, a better result, a healthier outcome, then it should be encouraged. But for that to happen what is often required is for one person to take him- or herself out of the argument and act as a facilitator, someone who keeps the argument on track and emotions under control. It takes a little effort sometimes, but it makes such a huge difference. *Blessed are the peacemakers.*

And what should we do about the second, more destructive, form of arguing – whatever the topic? Well, ideally, that should be stopped by the boss or HR – but it may also have to be us if they don't, won't, or can't act. Again, *Blessed are the peacemakers*. We may not want to get involved in the argument, we may feel it's none of our business, we may feel that we'll become the next target. But keeping the peace is a pretty serious responsibility, so with sensitivity (and without self-righteousness) we should try to define the situation. Perhaps humour will help. Perhaps listening – really listening – to what the argumentative person is saying will help us get to the root of their problem. And, perhaps, there is a real problem, and the complaints, the arguments, need to be channelled in a different way through to management. Again, the bottom line here is loving our neighbour: both the one doing the arguing and those who are on the receiving end of it. And, again, making the workplace into a place where we can cooperate to build something that matters, something that's important to God.

But what about that third type of argument – the righteous argument? Here I am cautious to the point of suspicion, but I also acknowledge that we may have a duty as Christians sometimes to make and even encourage such arguments. Why am I suspicious? Well, we touched a little on this in the chapter on what to do if asked to act against our Christian beliefs. What it boils down to is that as humans we are forever trying to cloak ourselves in the mantle of God's righteousness. And we do find very attractive some of God's tasks – particularly that of judging our fellow humans. Once we convince ourselves that something is wrong, our anger can turn from righteous to self-righteous very quickly. Or, put slightly differently, our passion for justice can very easily, and quickly, become a passion for judgment – and that becomes about power with all the possibilities that brings for a myriad of wrong turns. "Judge not, lest ye be judged" gives us a very practical reason for not falling into this trap (Matthew 7:1 KJV). But it is the damage we do to ourselves, to our relationships with others and with God that should really worry us. Once we are judging, we are no longer treating the other as a fully equal human.

But, my concerns aside, what if it really is necessary to argue over some injustice large or small? Let's look at it in a slightly different way. What if you feel you've been badly or unfairly treated? If you're in a very small business, you may have to try to sort it out with your boss, or walk away. But if your business is large enough, there will almost certainly be some type of internal grievance procedure that will take you through a series of steps to try to resolve the issue. It can be a good thing because it takes the direct confrontation out of the picture. Statements are made, interviews taken and so on. It can feel impersonal, and it's not perfect. You can still feel the system is stacked against you. But the HR folks have an interest in making sure you have no possible procedural complaints. Nevertheless, we should still be a little careful in utilizing these structures. I do remember a colleague from one of my government jobs who often felt very aggrieved and had frequent recourse to the grievance procedures. That colleague may or may not have been badly treated by senior management, but by putting themselves into the process (which took a lot of time – and a lot of physical and emotional energy) they locked themselves, on an almost permanent basis, into a problem which might better have been let go. Why let go? Because in the end it affected them most and tied up so much of their emotional life. Again, some things are worth arguing over – but the fact you may have an argument to make isn't the full answer as to whether you should actually pursue it. The threshold questions should always be: what will best promote healing; what in the end is going to make me happier;

and what is going to give me the most time to spend fruitfully, whether it's with family, friends, or with God?

Moving on, in a slightly different category, what if the matter is not about you but about something the company has done, or in some way sanctioned? Something possibly criminal, or at least a legal or regulatory violation? Well, again, if your company is small, then you may need to go straight to the police, or at least go and talk to a lawyer or a body like the Citizens Advice Bureau. But if your business is larger, then every well-run company should have a whistle-blower procedure. Let me be very clear. If something wrong has been done, then I think you have an absolute obligation to blow the whistle on that. No sense of misguided loyalty to your colleagues (or even timidity) should prevent you from arguing what you believe to be true. If the business is engaged in illegal or unethical activity, you have an obligation to do something about it. And, legal reasons apart, I would argue you also have a theological obligation because of the damage to the business and your fellow workers' ability to contribute to the ongoing act of creation. Some may call you a hero, and others a traitor. Probably, in fact, you're neither (and additional complications come your way if you get a reward for the whistle-blowing). However, I believe your obligation is completely straightforward. Blow the whistle.

But that can also be a tough and lonely road. There was an article in the *Financial Times* (5 June 2013) about whistle-blowers in the UK and the difficult time they've had. One, a very successful accountant, went to a large British bank, HBOS, to be head of risk in 2002. He alerted the board to what he thought was excessive risk taking and was fired for his troubles. For ten years no one would offer him a job. Things had started to look up in the months before the article was written, but it had been a very hard road. What really struck me, however, was that he said that it was only thanks to his wife that he had kept going. The day he was fired he went home and the first thing she said to him was: "Don't worry, it will be all right. It's all part of God's plan." That is faith – but it is not easy faith.[5]

So there can be a place for arguing in the workplace. It may often be the best way to a better result; it sometimes may be the only way to the truth. But, again, arguing is one of those things we need to consider carefully. As Jesus himself showed, there is a time to be argumentative when something really important is at stake. But we are also called upon to be peacemakers – whether by helping resolve other people's arguments or through not being argumentative ourselves. Sometimes arguing can be fun and sometimes too much fun. But if everyone's always arguing, the one thing we can be certain of is that the workplace itself will not be fun.

---

5 I have not mentioned any of the individual reactions to these chapters when originally given as talks, but I want to make this one exception because I know that many people have mixed views about whistle-blowers. By chance (it was, perhaps, just that Thursday, and, of course, St Martin's is on the Trafalgar Square tourist route), an American couple happened by to listen to this talk. Here's part of what the husband subsequently wrote to me: "I was a whistle-blower [in a significant US case] ... As you mention, it is a lonely road to travel. The reward/compensation I received was being downsized ... [I]t took me three and a half years to find another job. Fortunately God also gave me a loving wife to travel this road. I have always felt that God has been walking with me through difficult and good times." Make no mistake – to travel that road can take real courage.

17

What Happens If... I Have to Respond to a Difficult Email?[6]

Ephesians 4:26–27, 29–32 (NRSV)

Be angry but do not sin; do not let the sun go down on your anger, and do not make room for the devil... Let no evil talk come out of your mouths, but only what is useful for building up, as there is need, so that your words may give grace to those who hear. And do not grieve the Holy Spirit of God, with which you were marked with a seal for the day of redemption. Put away from you all bitterness and wrath and anger and wrangling and slander, together with all malice, and be kind to one another, tender-hearted, forgiving one another, as God in Christ has forgiven you.

When was it that we started to lose control of ourselves? I remember reading an article in one of the British Sunday newspapers, at least twenty years ago now, where someone – the Prince of Wales, I recall – was described as being "incandescent with rage". I remember being both worried and fascinated. Fascinated, because incandescent – previously a term I'd only applied to light bulbs

---

6   Or Facebook post, or SMS, or Tweet, or iMessage, or any other type of electronic communication...

– sounded much more serious (and, perhaps, intriguing) than something like "cross", "annoyed", or "irritated". Incandescent meant off-the-scale angry, nuclear, white hot. And I was worried for pretty much the same reasons. Incandescent seemed to take anger and ratchet it up several notches. If someone was irritated you might be able to soothe the irritation. If someone was agitated you might be able to calm them down. Even anger might be amenable to discussion and reasoning. But incandescent? Either the bulb popped or you had to break it. There was simply no way back from incandescent. It seemed to take anger to a new – but, apparently, acceptable – height.

So, what was going on? The press trying to spice up an otherwise boring royal story? A more general shift, as we were moving into an age of 24-hour TV, which meant that in order to get and keep people's attention something needed to be made to sound more exciting? Perhaps a foreshadowing of the hugely increased information flow that the internet would bring? Perhaps a slow loosening of impulse control that started in the 1960s? Or, perhaps, some combination of all of the above? In any event, in the past twenty years as the speed of information delivery has increased, so has our need – or perceived need – to respond to it quickly.

Now there is something quite un-Christian about this. Starting with Jesus, and followed by the church ever since, the need for contemplation, for prayer, for unhurried action is emphasized as necessary for our development as full human beings, for discerning the will of God, for finding God Himself. And this is not just for monks in monasteries or priests in churches, but for the whole people of God – for those of us who work in businesses large and small. And yet, that world that so many of us live in is one where that type of extended contemplation is near impossible – in many ways a lot more difficult than it was even twenty years ago. We have to – or, at least, have to have the capacity to – respond ever quicker. There's evidence that this jagged, fast, relentless activity is re-wiring our brains, so that we respond to this information surge in many ways like drug or alcohol addicts.

In a way, emails stand as one of the clearest symbols of this change. In some respects they maintain the form of older means of communication: they're written, sometimes to look like letters, by one person and sent to another; they're called "mail"; they arrive in "mailboxes". But, of course, they're also very different. If someone sends you one, it arrives immediately and you can reply within seconds, and it will be received by the sender only seconds after that. You don't have to get out a pen and find some paper. You don't have to put a stamp on an envelope and go to the postbox. And once it's sent, it has gone. But it remains in electronic form forever. It can be sent to the whole world, forwarded time and time again. You could say the same about the phone, but there you actually have to dial a number, find the person in, and then speak to that other person, and make some type of human contact influenced by the other person's voice, their mood. And, unless the call is being recorded, it's less permanent. But with emails, the human contact is minimal.

And then there's the number of them. I get around 150 a day – far too many to read, far less respond to, in a considered way. And yet the expectation is that they will be answered almost immediately. So here we have – to use a cliché – the "perfect storm" of the information age. More information than we can handle; no time for reflection; an almost effortless, but profoundly impersonal means of communication unrestrained by having to raise anything more than a finger; and a means of communication unrestrained by the human discipline of looking someone in the eye or hearing their voice. In the fast-moving, pressured environment that many workplaces are, it's inevitable that some emails are going to sound terse, or rude, or insulting. And the temptation is to reply – instantaneously – in the same vein. Without even the 30 seconds for reflection that getting up from your workstation and walking over to the other person would provide, you can shoot off an unconsidered, unfiltered, and totally permanent, un-erasable reply. It may not be the email that brings down the company – although that can happen – but it may wound or insult and thereby impair harmony and cooperation in the workplace. And that is the opposite of loving our neighbour, the opposite of participating with God in the healing of creation.

So how do we deal with the difficult email in an environment where everything seems to compel an immediate response? It's tough, but the good news is that if we can find an answer to this, we may be able to answer the broader question of how it is possible to be reflective in today's workplace. As mentioned in the last chapter, I think a lot of this comes down to what we might loosely call "anger management". And on this subject Paul is very useful indeed. He tells us first that anger can be justified, but that we should not sin. This must be "righteous anger" – and this will be quite rare outside narrow boundaries (and, again, we must be very careful not to cloak our own petty concerns with this righteousness). But even if our anger is righteous, we should not let the sun go down on that anger. In other words, we should not let the anger burrow into us and change our personalities. If we do that, then, as Paul says, we open ourselves up to the possibility of evil, or "the devil" in his words, coming into us because of the change that the deforming nature of anger can bring about. So stewing, letting the anger brew and simmer, is a bad thing. But does that mean we should just fire off an angry email and then forget about it, on the basis that we're not letting the sun go down on that anger?

Well, perhaps not. Paul goes on to say: "Let no evil talk come out of your mouths, but only what is useful for building up, as there is need, so that your words may give grace to those who hear." In other words, while righteous anger might be acceptable as long as it results in "building up", anything that does not build up will not be. And that's where many emails will fall down for the reasons we have already discussed – the lack of human contact, their instantaneousness, and so on. So we need to be thinking about how – unless a really important point of principle is involved, something that will rise to the level of righteousness – we should be replying in a way that will build up, not pull down.

What does this mean? Well Paul then goes on immediately to say: "Put away from you all bitterness and wrath and anger and wrangling and slander, together with all malice, and be kind to one another, tender-hearted, forgiving one another, as God in Christ has forgiven you." And so, once again, here is the Christian answer. Unless something absolutely critical, something absolutely central is at stake, our job is to be the peacemaker, not the righteous militant. Obviously that can be hard to do sometimes. If that annoying colleague sends the supremely annoying email, it is so, so tempting just to shoot back in similar fashion. But that's wrong. It falls squarely into diving into the wrath, bitterness, anger, wrangling, slander, and malice that Paul tells us to keep away from – all those things that can deform us.

So, in practical terms what can we do? Well, I think there are both some negative things and some positive ones. The negative, perhaps, seem obvious. If one of the major problems of email is the ability to reply at once, then step away from the computer. Set rules. Always count to ten. Go for a short walk before replying to a difficult email. Store it in your draft emails for at least an hour (or better overnight). Never, ever send a reply late in the evening. And never, ever after you've had a drink. Simple – but they can be life savers. What you need to do is to give yourself the time to reflect on whether your reply builds up or pulls down. In other words, is the topic a truly critical one or simply peripheral? Is your anger righteous or personal? What will this do to workplace relationships and to work cooperation? Just allow a little space for reflection. Also think what might happen to that email after you've sent it. Who else might it also go to? And we might, finally, want to think about lesson number one learned at our mother's knee: if you can't think of something nice to say, then don't say anything.

So those are the negative rules. What might some of the positive actions be? Well, here we might go back to the peacemaker roles and to Jesus' statement about turning the other cheek. That slightly misunderstood latter phrase is often read as a literal – and slightly preachy – injunction to passively sit back and allow ourselves to be hit again. But I think it can be better understood as an injunction to try to reach out again to others who have hurt us, scorned us, even if there is a real chance that they will do it again. So we might take the opportunity in replying to the difficult email to try to reach out to the person who sent it. To try to understand their point of view. To suggest a solution in which they won't lose face. Maybe we also offer to meet for coffee or for lunch. In other words, we make a positive effort to try to restore, to heal, the relationship. One of our goals as Christians is to break cycles of violence, of negativity, where one angry act feeds another angry act in a never-ending, often worsening cycle. If we try to break that cycle by sending a completely different email – different in tone and motivation, opening up new possibilities – then we will have actually done something profoundly Christian.

But let me also suggest something which may sound radical or perhaps just bizarre in our wired world. Don't reply to the email at all. Instead, if the person is in the workplace, how about actually getting up from your desk and going and talking to that person? How about some real interaction? Of course, sometimes the email you received may be so difficult or so inflammatory that going to see the person will make things even worse, and then you need to think of other ways (and perhaps with other people) of defusing the situation. But much more often, it's just a question of going to see the other person that overcomes all of the disadvantages we've talked about earlier: the impersonal nature, the lack of human contact, the harshness of words on a page, the permanence of the reply, etc., etc. When we're with another person, able to read their body language, their mood, we have the chance to adapt, to feel our way towards a solution that email almost never allows.

And if they're not in the workplace, then pick up the phone – or even better these days, try a videoconference so you can see their face and hear their voice, even if it's not as good as actually being with them. Again, there is some element of human contact that avoids some of the problems of email. The key thing to remember is that we are not obliged to respond in exactly the same way, or medium, in which we have been approached. Simply because someone has sent us an email does not mean we have to respond by email. We must not be trapped in that way. In the cause of trying to heal, to improve the workplace, we should be inventive.

I still think emails are, on balance, a true net positive. They allow many more opportunities for communication than before. But they do come with dangers, both inside the workplace and out. I think we can enhance the positives and reduce the negatives – even in the case of difficult emails –

if we remember that as human beings we are meant to be in relationship, personal relationship, with those about us (and with God). So if we can reply to that difficult email in a way that enhances a relationship, then we should do that. If we can't, then we should find some other way to respond. It's not about becoming incandescent. It's not about always escalating.

As one final sanity check I'd recommend applying the Golden Rule: do to others as you would have them do to you. Think, before you hit the "send" button, *How would I feel if I got this reply? What reaction would it provoke in me, good or bad?* Put slightly differently, in Paul's terms, would this reply "build up... so that your words may give grace to those who hear"? That should always be our test before we send our permanent, irretrievable, irreversible electronic reply out into the ether.

18

What Happens If... My Boss Asks Me to Lie?

Matthew 10:7–11, 16 (NRSV)

"As you go, proclaim the good news, 'The kingdom of heaven has come near.' Cure the sick, raise the dead, cleanse the lepers, cast out demons. You received without payment; give without payment. Take no gold, or silver, or copper in your belts, no bag for your journey, or two tunics, or sandals, or a staff; for labourers deserve their food. Whatever town or village you enter, find out who in it is worthy, and stay there until you leave... See, I am sending you out like sheep into the midst of wolves; so be wise as serpents and innocent as doves."

I suspect your view of this question about lying may be coloured – as mine certainly is – by movies of a certain type. It might be about a crooked law firm; it may be about an industrial giant secretly dumping toxic waste; it may be about a pharmaceutical company which hides evidence of the harm that its blockbuster drug can inflict; it may be about cigarette companies hiding the evidence of addiction and disease that their products cause; or it may be about the big bank or brokerage firm that hides the illegal trades or evidence of dodgy products that they've been selling to unsuspecting consumers. There's always a scene where the boss – whether they're a silver-haired Richard Gere or someone much less prepossessing – faces the much younger, and always idealistic, new recruit, and asks them to lie for the company. Most often (though not always) after a bit of a wobble the young hero decides to buck the firm, give up a life of promised wealth and comfort, and serve the public good. We all leave the cinema secure in the knowledge that we would do exactly the same. But would we?

In 1944 C. S. Lewis, in a famous speech called "The Inner Ring", at King's College London, spoke about a certain type of corruption. In order to please those on the inside, in order to stay a member of the inside, all one is required to do is to utter one small, almost completely insignificant, lie – an utterly immaterial moral shading. Nothing more. Something so close to the borderline that it really could fall on either side of that line. And then perhaps just another very small one to stay in the inner ring. And then just another little one, and another, and another, until, in Lewis's words, we go bad. It's an almost imperceptible progression. And a common one, because, in fact, we're often not faced with telling one big lie that takes us straight from being very good to being very bad in one go. More often it is with these small, almost indiscernible, moves that at a certain point along the way we suddenly realize that we are well over the boundary and already in trouble. And what do we then do when faced with the sick realization that in fact we're not facing a clean decision between staying good and turning bad, but a decision between having already turned bad and getting still worse? I suspect that some of us would exercise our considerable human skills in rationalization and manage to convince ourselves that what we had done wasn't so bad, and nor will the next step be either. Or that we need to do it to keep food on the table. Or that we need to do it to stay in the company to fight the next battle against a much greater evil. Or that we're scared.

So, in considering this question – the "Would we?" question – I think we need to be a little more humble and a little more realistic. We've looked before at Richard Rohr and his idea of living "on the edge of the inside" as a place where we constantly question our business and our motives. That can work as long as we practise the questioning each and every day. Whether or not you truly believe in sin and evil, most humans have a tendency to head for comfort and security rather than difficulty and insecurity. That's not to criticize or to judge, but if we're not to fall victim to the compass turning one degree at a time until we find ourselves 180 degrees from where we should be, we need to be constantly vigilant.

And we should remember that lies need not always be positive acts of deceit – saying that something happened or someone did something even when they didn't. An omission may also add up to a lie. In business, this might often be the more frequent case. "Just forget to mention that one small number," you may be told. "Just forget to mention that one almost irrelevant fact." As we'll discuss in a moment, there may be occasions where the bare unvarnished truth is not a kindness, and a little shading does better preserve our human relationships. But generally, these lies of omission can be just as damaging as positive acts. So we need to be aware of that temptation which, in any number of rationalizations, can seem less offensive: after all we're not actively telling a lie, right, we're just not telling the complete truth...

So what happens if we find we've already crossed the line? Should we just carry on, or instead somehow try to turn back? Here I have to be careful not to sound too preachy or too Protestant. But one of the problems with sin, as we'll discuss in much more detail in the next two chapters, is that it feeds on itself to grow stronger. It's a bit like cheating on a diet or having a cigarette when you've given up. Once you've broken the rule, you feel you may as well go all the way. That's what sin does to us; but the way out of this is that God, in the form of Jesus Christ, died on the cross to save us from all of these sins for all time. We are redeemed – if we wish to be. So at any point, whichever side of the line we may be on, God is ready to welcome us back without punishment or reproach – in fact, with rejoicing and celebration. That's not to say we won't face human punishment – we may – but in the really important relationships with God, and with our fellow humans, we will be back in the right place. That may still not be easy – the parable of the Prodigal Son, for example, shows that the seeking of redemption can be hard – but the gift is always available.

So that's the first question – would we always make the ethical, clear-cut decision to refuse the boss's invitation to lie? Perhaps not as often as we might like to think. But there is, perhaps, a second question. Is lying always wrong? Should we always refuse to lie? Now, to be very clear, in many cases the obvious answer is going to be "yes". We should not do things that harm the environment, the public, the customer, our fellow employees, or even, a little more abstractly, "the system". But it's worth asking the question, because it goes to the issue of what a lie is.

Might lying ever be justified? Well, let me start with an easy hypothetical. One of your colleagues has experienced a personal tragedy. As a result his work has become pretty haphazard. But your boss wants to see him through a tough period, so she asks you to go tell your colleague what a fabulous job he's doing. It's clearly not true – but I'm guessing most of us would do it. Let's take another slightly more complicated one. You find out that one of your colleagues is doing something illegal, so you let your boss know. But it turns out he already knows and has almost enough evidence to go to the police. So he asks you to lie to your colleague so he won't realize you're on to him. Justified? Again, I think most would say yes. So, lying might not always be bad. A lie might always be an untruth, or less than the whole truth, but it might not always be "wrong".

Before we go too much further down this route, however, let's look at the Bible. The New Testament is forthright in its condemnation of lying – although I'll return to our reading in a moment. The Old Testament is a little more mixed. Obviously, the ninth of the Ten Commandments forbids the bearing of false witness against your neighbour, and this has been broadly interpreted as a prohibition on all types of lying. And there are plenty of other similar passages. Take this one, for example, from Proverbs, where it says that God hates "haughty eyes, a lying tongue, and hands that shed innocent blood, a heart that devises wicked plans, feet that hurry to run to evil, [and] a lying witness who testifies falsely" (Proverbs 6:17–19 NRSV). But there are also stories about some of the great biblical figures practising deception – which is to say, lying. Abraham, the great patriarch, passed his wife off as his sister not just once but twice in tricky situations. The Hebrew midwives, told by the Egyptian Pharaoh to kill any boy born to an Israelite, made up a complete lie in order not to do that. David asked Saul's son Jonathan to tell lies for him. And then, of course, there's Jacob, whom we discussed above, who dressed up like his brother Esau and lied to his father Isaac, in order to steal his father's blessing. Yet God met Jacob in the wilderness, where the ladder touched down from heaven to earth and made Jacob a series of remarkable promises for him and his descendants. Behold, I am with you, God said, and will keep you wherever you go.

So what do we take from this? Well, I don't think it means that if you're otherwise a great guy, then it's all right if you lie. But perhaps there's something about the nature or the purpose of the untruth which we need to think about. Let's go back to the ninth commandment. It prohibits the bearing of false witness against our neighbour. In other words, it prohibits something that damages our neighbour. It is, therefore, a complement to the positive commandment to love our neighbour. So a lie that hurts people, or damages the world, or otherwise has a negative effect is prohibited. In one way or another, it damages God's creation, and that's bad.

But there's more danger and damage in a lie than just hurting others. We also need to be aware that some lies may hurt only us – the ones we tell to ourselves about our own motives, our own loves, our own fears. These lies may not hurt others directly, but they can still twist us out of shape, and lead us into darker places. They damage our relationships with everyone around us and especially with God. Even if we tell ourselves we're not damaging someone else, if we become inured to the difference between right and wrong we nevertheless dull something deep within us. Those lies are dangerous, too. So it is to both purpose and effect we must look in evaluating the danger and the damage of any lie.

Let's go back to the question I actually posed: What do we do if our boss asks us to lie? That may seem like a pretty binary choice: we tell him we will lie, or we tell him we won't lie. But are those really the only options? If we follow either of those then there is the danger we damage ourselves. In the first instance, we diminish ourselves by telling the lie. In the second case we may, at the very least, put our job at risk. But what if we seek to turn this bad opportunity into a good one? In our Bible passage, Jesus instructs the apostles as they go out into the world. Their job, as is ours, is to proclaim the gospel and minister to the outcasts. He warns them of trouble to come and advises them to be "wise as serpents ['cunning' in some translations] and innocent as doves". I don't think this is an invitation to lie, but I do think it is an invitation to be inventive in dealing with difficult situations. Sometimes it may be necessary to tell the truth, to tell it out loud, and to tell it at any cost – and I referred in an earlier chapter to the importance of whistle-blowing. But as with all dramatic, public, righteous actions, with potentially far-reaching effects, we should carefully analyse the case first. And in some circumstances we may want to consider other possibilities.

Perhaps our boss is under pressure at work or at home. He's desperate to get out from under that pressure and so he concocts a lie and tries to make us a partner in it. But perhaps there's another solution he's missed, or perhaps the situation is not as bad as he thinks. In that case we can help him out of the hole he's dug for himself without compromising ourselves. And in fact we may have done more than that, because we will also have saved him from himself, and from damage being done to God's act of creation in the workplace. Or perhaps there is no way out, but you can persuade her that together you can face it and deal with the consequences, with the fallout from whatever it was that your boss was hoping to lie her way around. Or, another way, which might be slightly more "wise" or "cunning", could be to agree to tell the lie, but then not do it. Perhaps the crisis passes and you can then reveal your own lie to your boss. Perhaps the crisis doesn't pass, but you then explain to your boss why you thought it best to do what you did. These are only a couple of examples, but they shed a little more light on this than just the simple alternative of yes and no. And they show the possibilities of being able to get something good out of something which on the surface appears to offer only bad alternatives.

So, to return to the beginning, the dilemma may not be as clear-cut as it at first appears. We need to consider both motives and results. But the thing we need to worry about most is not the big, obvious, movie-style choice between telling the big lie or staying good. What should concern us most is the small, little untruths that slowly propel towards and then over the line. And it is to that issue that we'll return in the next chapter.

19

What Happens If... I'm Tempted to Do Something Bad in the Workplace?

1 Corinthians 10:12–13 (ESV)

Therefore let anyone who thinks that he stands take heed lest he fall. No temptation has overtaken you that is not common to man. God is faithful, and he will not let you be tempted beyond your ability, but with the temptation he will also provide the way of escape, that you may be able to endure it.

There's one of those Oscar Wilde aphorisms that often gets wheeled out when people talk about this subject: "I can resist everything except temptation." It's snappy, quite amusing, and, as it happens, totally unhelpful. Don't worry. I'm not going to spend the rest of this chapter lecturing you on the weakness of humankind and our inability to withstand temptation. But temptation is not something we can brush aside with an ineffective aphorism. We need to understand how serious temptation is and the damage that it can do to us and to others. As Paul says in our Bible passage, we need to be very aware of the power of the temptation in order not to succumb to it. It should be said, of course, that many of the temptations that we worry about endlessly as a church –

particularly sexual ones – are often precisely the temptations that we really needn't worry about too much (even if turning them into collective obsessions proves irresistible). But many of the temptations offered in the workplace actually are rather serious, and we need to be aware of them and examine how we might resist them or, even better, subvert them.

But what, you may be wondering, am I talking about? What are these temptations in the workplace? The desire to take things home from the stationery cupboard; to claim reimbursement for a personal taxi fare; or, perhaps, some type of sexual attraction to a fellow worker? Is that really so very bad, you might ask? Perhaps, perhaps not. But the real dangers in the workplace lie elsewhere. They lie in the way that the structure of the business works; they lie in the way we are expected to achieve results; they lie in the hierarchy; they lie in the compensation system. In other words, the workplace does present all of the big temptations that the Bible spends a lot of time talking about.

In the workplace lie the temptations of power and the exercise of that power to control and dominate others. The lure of money and riches, and the perversion that that causes, which can rot the very core of our being. The striving for success at any cost, even if it means trampling over our neighbour to get there and abandoning even the most basic ethical principles along the way. The thrill of the chase, the adrenalin rush that requires us continually to go faster, further, harder. The abandonment of family and friends, and of thought and reflection. And the abandonment of God. Those are the temptations that the workplace offers. I defy you to tell me they're not serious.

But if you think I'm exaggerating, you may want to take a quick look at the 2013 UK Parliamentary report on Banks and Financial Crisis by the Parliamentary Commission on

Banking Standards.[7] It makes sobering reading as it talks about compensation encouraging misconduct, about the rewards of excessive short-term risk taking, and about the lack of personal responsibility from the most senior executives down. These might seem legal or regulatory matters, and of course they are. But they also go to questions of behaviour, about how we conduct ourselves, and how we treat others. So these are not just legal issues; they're also theological because they go to the heart of what it means to be human, how we relate to our God, and what we do about our own frailty and the attractiveness of temptation.

So what are we to do? Well, I imagine you'd expect me to say a number of things at this stage. A simple point, perhaps, about loving our neighbour, which should give us pause before we give into the temptation that will hurt that neighbour. The need for humility, and the point that Jesus makes constantly about the first being last, and the last being first – in other words, about the need not to get hung up on our own status which can cause us to trample over others. Or, perhaps, something about the Pharisees and lawyers who were supposedly the leaders of society yet looked for personal glorification and enriched themselves. Or one of my favourite parables (mentioned in Chapter 8) about the man who built bigger barns to house the increased harvest that God had given him, rather than sharing it with others – a parable, in other words, about a sense of proportion, an acknowledgment of when we have enough or even more than we might need. And finally – although there are scores of similar ones that we could draw on – the story of Dives and Lazarus. Only when he is roasting in hell does Dives, the rich man, realize too late what he should have been doing in his own lifetime.

---

7   http://www.publications.parliament.uk/pa/jt201314/jtselect/jtpcbs/27/2703.htm (June 2013)

But I'm not going to focus on those. There's nothing wrong with them; they are all, clearly, appropriate biblical messages – but they're also unremittingly negative. In one way or another they all come down to "Thou shalt not…" And there's a big problem with that. It's this: however valid the message might be, it turns non-churchgoing people off. "There they go again," they say. "Not content with stigmatizing various aspects of sexuality and trying to keep out women bishops, they always bang on about punishment and hellfire." So, as Christians, if we want to get across our message on dealing with temptation in the workplace – if we want to make a real difference – we're going to have to find a very different way of talking about it.

Don't get me wrong. Judgment and a fear of some type of ultimate reckoning with God are a necessary underpinning of our faith. But I do believe that the thrust of Christianity is really in another and more hopeful direction. It's about healing creation and building up the kingdom. It's about living fuller and more fulfilled lives, both individually and in relationship with others in community. It's about celebrating when we find the lost coin; it's about trading everything else we have for the pearl of great price. It's about the knowledge that whenever we fall backwards God is waiting to catch us. It's the knowledge that a good act may lead to another. In other words it's about a series of "do's" rather than a series of "don'ts" – but a series of "do's" that we undertake because we want to, not because someone makes us. Life shouldn't be about wondering how soon we're going to mess up again and get punished. It should be about knowing that when we next mess up, God will still love us.

I'm using a lot of words, but the picture I'm trying to paint is that life is not about keeping our noses clean or not getting caught. It's not about putting ourselves in a situation where temptation will never arise. It is about interacting with people, getting joy from them; about seeing the cloud's silver lining even when we know it's pouring and we're getting wet. And it's about facing temptation in the world, and winning. So, yes, I still believe in judgment and a condition, a situation, where there may be a "wailing and gnashing of teeth" (to use Jesus' own words). But I am even more certain that that is not what God wants for us – it's something that we do to ourselves.

So, at least to my way of thinking, temptations, whether in the workplace or anywhere else, are not like an endless series of hidden speed traps where you clock up the penalty points that could eventually send you to hell. No, I think that temptations are the cracks and fissures in the surface of our imperfect world, which the love of God enables us, time and time again, to jump over without hurting ourselves. And that's what Paul talks about in this chapter's reading. Temptations will come and we will be tested, but never beyond what we can bear, and God will always be there to help us.

So what does this mean? How do we take this positive stand on temptation? Well, I want to talk about some practical things relating to power, hierarchy, and money in the workplace. All of these features score low marks on most people's "good Christian" scale and yet – as we noted at the beginning – they are an integral part of the workplace. So we are left with the option of walking away from all of them – and perhaps from business itself – or of staying in the mire and trying to do something with these. I don't think we should walk away, so I'd like to look for positives to help us resist the temptation that power, hierarchy, and money offer, rather than a series of "thou shalt nots". That strikes me as the way that God enables us, as Paul says, to withstand temptation. Not through a series of prohibitions requiring superhuman willpower, but through the ability to turn those temptations into a different course.

Let's start with power. As a schoolboy I learned Lord Acton's famous dictum that "all power corrupts, and absolute power corrupts absolutely". So power is dangerous, a sort of live electric current, and we do have to be very careful with it. But if we find ourselves in possession of it do we walk away from it, or do we try to resist that corruption, that temptation? Power can, clearly, be used positively. Think of two now fairly uncontroversial examples: FDR's "New Deal" in the US in the 1930s and the British Labour government after 1945. In both cases, whatever you might think of some of the economic policies involved, the use of governmental authority to create jobs for the unemployed and to provide a safety net for the poor and the old was – wherever on the political spectrum you come from – an enormously beneficial use of power. So, to take it to our context, you could use your power in your workplace to change your business model, to pay more attention to your employees or to the environment.

So on one level, power, responsibly exercised, can have broad societal benefits. But there is also the personal aspect – how do we avoid becoming seduced by the exercise of power, even in a good cause? Well, there we have to try to detach our personality, our estimation of ourselves, from that power – rather than letting them become commingled. We can do that by sharing it or delegating it, by voluntarily limiting its scope, or by only exercising it for a limited period and then stepping down. To resist the temptation of power we should be sure that we are exercising it in a beneficial, not selfish, way. And we must be very clear that we only temporarily exercise the power that has been given to us and that will again flow away from us. It is not something that we deserve, or have created, or that is part of us.

And what about hierarchy? Well, again, hierarchies are one of those things that exist in human society. Most historical attempts at living in complete equality have quickly collapsed, often leading to new, and sometimes more rigid, even vicious, hierarchies. Other experiments have indeed reduced inequality and flattened hierarchies, but at staggering human cost – think of some Communist regimes such as the Khmer Rouge in Cambodia. So again, how can we use hierarchy in a good way? Well, to the extent that hierarchy interacts with power, and exalted position can be used for beneficial purposes, we should use status in that way. And a position in a hierarchy can also be used to promote and reward good behaviour. But again we need to be very careful that we don't confuse our position, our status, with who we actually are (and who God wants us to be).

Our primary identity is not as Director of this, or Vice-President of that. It's as a human, friend, parent, child (of our parents, and of God). So, we need to keep hierarchy and our place in it at arm's length. How might we do that? Perhaps by subverting it, by making gentle fun of it, by showing (and believing) that while this is the current structure of things, we see its absurdity. Or we can seek to make the hierarchy much more fluid, so that neither we nor anyone else fix ourselves in a certain place or position in it as a statement about ourselves. And a corollary of that is that sometimes we might take a step down in the hierarchy to demonstrate that where we are in that structure at any particular point doesn't say anything about our value or self-worth. Again, if we do these things then we might be able to get something positive out of hierarchy both for a broader community as well as for ourselves, rather than giving in to its temptations.

And, finally, money – Mammon – that thing which we cannot serve if we also want to serve the Living God. Money is also clearly dangerous, and its temptations can lead us in many perilous directions: away from families, against fellow workers, into relatively useless but highly rewarded activity. However, we should also remember that money is in one sense neutral. It is merely a means of exchange. It is what we do to money, and what it does to us, that turns it into a bad thing. But money can also be used to do amazing things: to build buildings like St Martin-in-the-Fields; to provide for care and outreach to the homeless; to finance cures for disease. So how do we deal with the temptations of money in the workplace, again seeking positive ways rather than prohibitions?

Well, at the collective – the workplace – level, one way is by sending messages about the good uses of money. This could be a charity that the business supports, or a proportion of profits that go to a good cause, or a corporate commitment to distribute rewards inside the workplace that narrow rather than widen inequality. In relation to that last one, not every large business can be an employee-owned partnership.[8] But despite that, a more cooperative model could be replicated in other management structures through changes to the compensation system to reduce the level of recognition and validation vested in the single, bald salary number.

And what about not getting captured by money on an individual level? Again, as with hierarchy, we should not use money to measure ourselves. Now that sounds a bit like "thou shalt not". So here's a more positive idea: give some away. Money can exercise a frightening grip on us – and an ever-tightening grip as we grow older and acquire more and more responsibilities. However much we have, it never feels like quite enough. The mortgage, the kids, the pension, something else – anything else. We always feel we need more. But if we give it away, even a little, we will realize that, in fact, we have more than we need, not less. We can do great things with it, give it to great causes. And suddenly we realize that life isn't

---

8   Although the John Lewis Partnership is a much-cited example in the UK.

about money; it's really about living with other people, caring for them – family, friends, neighbours. And it's also about liking what we do because it's actually enjoyable, because it actually contributes with God to the healing of creation.

So we can certainly be po-faced about temptation, and exhort ourselves and others not to do this, that, or the other – and then go on, almost inevitably, to fail in one respect or another. Or, while still being acutely aware of the danger, we can instead look the temptation straight in the eye and try to subvert it into something good, something positive. As Paul tells us, we will never be tempted more than we can bear – and subverting that temptation may turn out to be the way that God has given us to resist it. We can protect ourselves from the personal temptations offered by power, hierarchy, and money by ensuring that we don't let them get inside us. And we can also redirect them to serve beneficial ends, rather than selfish ones, when it comes to community.

It needs imagination and vigilance, but if we can redirect these temptations into a positive cause, then we will have done much, much more good than we would ever have done by walking away from them. Because instead of abandoning our murky, grimy, ambiguous workplace and its temptations in an attempt to keep ourselves pure and clean, we will have stayed and helped to improve the real world that God created and still loves.

20

What Happens If... I Do Something Bad in the Workplace?

Colossians 1:11–14, 19–20 (NRSV)

May you be made strong with all the strength that comes from his glorious power, and may you be prepared to endure everything with patience, while joyfully giving thanks to the Father, who has enabled you to share in the inheritance of the saints in the light. He has rescued us from the power of darkness and transferred us into the kingdom of his beloved Son, in whom we have redemption, the forgiveness of sins... For in him all the fullness of God was pleased to dwell, and through him God was pleased to reconcile to himself all things, whether on earth or in heaven, by making peace through the blood of his cross.

In the narrative we construct of our own life story, we are rarely the fool, or the bully, or the incompetent, or the manipulator, or the guilty party. That's always someone else – in fact, during the course of our lives many "someone else's", but almost never us. And yet, I suspect, most other people also feel that way, which raises the question of exactly who all those fools and bullies, all the incompetents, manipulators and the guilty, actually are. Our capacity to rewrite our own history is remarkable, and some would say that in order to be able to deal with the bad things life throws at us we need that ability. Well, maybe. But certainly when it comes to bad things we have done, it's really damaging. Damaging for others, of course, if we refuse to acknowledge what we have done and if we refuse to change – but also potentially deeply damaging to us. Why? Because we carry these wrongs, these little bits of guilt, around with us, and like barnacles on a rock the little pieces slowly build up until the natural surface is completely covered and it becomes something else. Guilt sticks; and guilt changes us.

The themes that we've looked at in this second section have mostly been about dilemmas that we might face in the workplace, and how to ensure a good outcome – an outcome that may reveal God to us and to others in the workplace, and an outcome that furthers God's creative work in that place (and, thus, in the world). In the previous chapter we looked at how we might subvert the temptations of power, money, and hierarchy in the workplace. We've also talked about how to avoid lying when asked to. About not working harder and harder so we damage neither our families nor our relationship with God. We've talked about loving our neighbour – the person in the cubicle next to us. About making – and demonstrating – ethical decisions in the workplace. About possible sins of commission – and also sins of omission.

But whatever we tell ourselves, however hard we try, do we always avoid the missteps, the foot faults? Do we sometimes fail? I defy you to tell me you – we, I – don't. And yet we rarely come clean about it. The barnacles on the rock continue to accumulate, obscuring who we really are, who we could really be. Well over thirty years after I left school, there are things that still make me squirm about boys I was mean to or the tricks I played on others. Those were sins of commission for the most part. More recently, in the context of the workplace, it has more been sins of omission: failing to comment on something that wasn't right; failing to stand up for someone, or against what someone else was doing. As I'm sure many of you also know, these events, these regrets, stay with you.

Now, I realize this all sounds a little gloomy, but there is some good news coming! The point is not that if we don't try hard enough we'll mess up. The point is that, as human beings, we will from time to time inevitably mess up, precisely because we are human beings. It's what happens when we meet this inevitable event – rather than how we always avoid it – that's the really interesting and important question. So what do we do when we mess up? Well, as already mentioned, we could just hide it from others (and from ourselves). But, at some level, we know what we've done. It may be a big thing or it may be a small thing, but whatever it us, there is an answer, and it's actually pretty simple – 'fess up, come clean, be honest. Name what it is you have done. But 'fess up to whom, you might be asking? Well, I think there are three distinct parts to that answer. As Christians, 'fess up to God. As members of a community (including a business community, a workplace) 'fess up to each other. And, as individuals, 'fess up to ourselves.

Let's start with God. Now 'fessing up to God requires us to get into the question of repentance. And the trouble with "repentance" is that it sounds both scary and utterly miserable. Sackcloth and ashes. A beating of the chest and endless mea culpas. But it needn't, and, in fact, it shouldn't be. We seem so often to forget one of the central, astonishing beliefs of Christianity. That belief is not – as I've tried to keep saying throughout this book – that there's an endless series of rules that we must stick to in order to be a Christian, failure to adhere to which will lead to us being thrown out of the club. No, this central, amazing belief is, as our Bible passage tells us, that the Son of God died on the cross to save us from our sins. All our sins: past, present, and future. Sins imagined, intended, contemplated, or completed. He died to save us from those stumbles, those foot-faults. All we will ever do is already forgiven. Think about it. He died to liberate us from our sin. Not so that we would never sin – be clear about that – but so that the mistakes we make, the temptations we succumb to, will not throw us into the outer darkness or into the "fires of hell".

But there's just one small catch. We have to be honest with God. The forgiveness is always totally, absolutely available. But for it to work, for its liberating power to run through us, we must acknowledge what has happened – not conceal it – and acknowledge our need of that forgiveness. Only if we are honest with God, only if we name what it is that we have done, can God take from us the bad, the wrong, the sin that He already died to save us from. But if we hold on to it, if we try to hide it from God and don't hand it over, if we try to cover our guilt in rich robes of community service, or extravagant displays of charity, then God will still not condemn us – but we will condemn ourselves. We will not be the living stones of the church, because we will instead be that barnacle-covered rock. But if we hold out that wrong to God – that elbowing ahead of a fellow worker; that malicious gossip; that hurt that our ambition has caused to our families; that distortion of our personality that the pursuit of money has brought – then the liberation will be able to start.

So that's 'fessing up to God. What about the second leg, 'fessing up to our fellow workers, to the community? Well, in some respects that may feel more difficult than a quick word with God. There are perhaps two separate elements to this 'fessing up. First, actually telling people that you've done something bad. Second, facing the consequences of that act, including, perhaps, punishment. Let me deal very quickly with the second. Saying sorry, 'fessing up, will always be enough to secure God's forgiveness, but it may not be enough to avoid earthly punishment. That may be profoundly uncomfortable, but repaying a debt to civil society – whether monetarily or through time served – is, as Paul makes clear, a legitimate price for societal cohesion. OK, enough of that.

But what about the first type of 'fessing up, about telling our fellow workers, those whom we may have hurt? Well, it's important to remember that repentance is not just a personal thing. We may view repentance through the lens of the movie camera: the quiet church, the rays of sunlight falling on the dark wood of the confessional box, the penance of fifty Hail Marys in front of the sun-dappled altar. But the death on the cross was not just to bring us individually into a place where our sins were forgiven and our relationship with God restored. It was also about restoring relationships between human beings, about restoring the community. About the healing of creation and advancing the kingdom that we have talked about before. About breaking the cycle of violence and sacrifice – and the cycle of deception that feeds those. As part of our acceptance of the gift of forgiveness for which Christ died, we also owe it to those whom we have hurt to let them know that we recognize what we have done and seek to make amends. That we recognize that they have laboured under a burden that we have placed on them – and which we now seek to take back and then hand on to God. That we recognize that the restoration of a relationship is more important than our saving face. In the same way that being honest with God is the way to restore our relationship with Him (enabling us to fully benefit from the gift His dying secured for us), being honest with our fellow workers, with those we have hurt, is a way of securing for the community, the workplace, the gift of forgiveness and the restoration of wholeness.

So what does this mean practically? Well, if we have gossiped about someone and hurt them, either in their own eyes or in the eyes of others, then we should tell them and apologize. And, as long as it does not impose further hurt, we might also tell them why we did it, why we hurt them. Perhaps because we felt weak ourselves and tried to clamber over them to popularity. Perhaps because we were jealous. Perhaps because things were going so badly for us that we wanted to drag someone else down to where we were (or thought we were). If we admit to these things, there will be the beginnings of healing for others, for the broader community, which is sustained by harmony not division, and for ourselves, unburdened of a weight we have been carrying. Or, if we have pushed people aside in our desire to secure promotion over them or more compensation than them, then we might tell them how we removed opportunity from them, about how we praised ourselves to our boss but denigrated them. About all the petty, spiteful things we did to make ourselves look good and them look bad. If we were successful in our machinations, we should look for ways to make amends – perhaps, for example, we might find a way of giving away any extra compensation we secured. Or, if we let work dominate our lives to the exclusion of all else, we might explain – confess – that to our spouse and to our children, and ask their forgiveness, too. To the spouse who had to bear all the burden at home because we were pursuing our own ambition. To the kids who missed out on a parent as they were growing up.

But again, this all sounds completely miserable. So, it's worth re-emphasizing right now – and again, and again, and again – that the point of this, the point of repentance, the point of saying sorry, the point of going through these difficult conversations, is to break out of the cage into which we've put ourselves (and, in the case of the workplace, into which we've put that community), in order for us and that community, or us and our family, to experience the freedom, the healing, the wholeness which is the forgiveness of sin. This is not about being miserable and punishing ourselves; it's about the joyful recognition and realization that we are none of us bound by the mistakes of our past, but rather always have the promise of the future. That is repentance and forgiveness – but the initial breaking of those bonds can be really, really hard.

And finally, we come to the 'fessing up to ourselves. In some respects, of course, in order to be able to 'fess up to God and to our fellow workers, we need to acknowledge the wrong, the bad thing done. But there's a little more to it than that. These are both externally focused. There does also need to be some internal focus. What do I mean by that? Well, again, there may be two aspects. One involves really, truly, naming the wrong and looking at its causes. But a second, equally important part involves forgiving ourselves. Only if we do both of those can we come closer not just to righting each past wrong, but to breaking the cycle which will otherwise almost inevitably lead us to do more bad things in the future.

So, first there's truly naming the wrong that we've done. Here our motives – or our understanding of what we've done – and not just our actions, need to be right. We may decide that we need to apologize – "seek repentance" – for something wrong. We may, however, also convince ourselves that what we did wasn't really too bad, but that we should ask God's forgiveness anyway as a sort of insurance policy. Or, perhaps, that while we weren't really bad, we should say sorry to our colleagues in order to improve the atmosphere in the workplace. Those aren't necessarily bad things to do, but neither are they effective – especially for us. We must certainly 'fess up to God and to our neighbour, but we must also be completely clear-eyed with ourselves about what it is we have done. And we must try to understand it. Why were we feeling so cruel that day? Why did we feel insecure? Why did we feel so spiteful? If this analysis makes us feel ashamed – well, so be it. That means we have understood it. But if we name it, if we objectify it, then we can examine it, consider it, demystify it. Whether it's something we did that we have to acknowledge as truly shocking, or something that has terrorized us unnecessarily, we are then in a position to ensure that that particular aspect of wrong is something we may be able to avoid doing again.

And that second thing – forgiving ourselves. This is one of the worst effects of doing wrong, doing something bad – "sinning", if we can use that rather old-fashioned word. It makes us feel dirty, unworthy, hateful. And in so doing, it makes it more likely that through self-loathing, or lack of self-esteem, we will do more wrong – because we believe ourselves to be trapped, already compromised, beyond redemption. But we never are – because that gift of forgiveness has already been secured. Once, for all, upon the cross. So forgiving ourselves comes back to the seemingly strange injunction in part of the Great Commandment – love your neighbour *as yourself*. As one of God's children, made in some way in His image, we are to reflect His love. And we don't do that by self-loathing. But escaping from that trap, from that vicious circle, requires us to admit to ourselves what we have done, to admit that alone we are incapable of doing anything about it, and then to throw ourselves upon – or perhaps into – the love of God. Forgiving ourselves is about letting God back in, about restoring wholeness. But that requires us to want to let God in, to want that wholeness, to want to love ourselves. And that all starts with complete and utter honesty to ourselves about the mess we're in and the help we need. Only then can we start to get out of it.

So we can and will go wrong, do something bad, in the workplace. But that is not the end. It may in fact be the beginning of something much better. We do need to 'fess up to God, to our co-workers in our workplace, and to ourselves. But if we do, then we may be able to move from the sterile self-righteousness of the Pharisees (which, of course, is always laced with a terrible fear of failing, of falling) to something much more creative, dynamic, alive. And there, in that place, by acknowledging our own weakness and inability to recover alone, we will be in a place where we are able to truly recognize, and accept, the gift of God's love in the forgiveness of all our sins bought for us on the cross.

PART III

Where is God at Work in the Bible?

21

The Talents

Matthew 25:14–30 (NRSV)

[Jesus said] "For it is as if a man, going on a journey, summoned his slaves and entrusted his property to them; to one he gave five talents, to another two, to another one, to each according to his ability. Then he went away. The one who had received the five talents went off at once and traded with them, and made five more talents. In the same way, the one who had the two talents made two more talents. But the one who had received the one talent went off and dug a hole in the ground and hid his master's money. After a long time the master of those slaves came and settled accounts with them. Then the one who had received the five talents came forward, bringing five more talents, saying, 'Master, you handed over to me five talents; see, I have made five more talents.' His master said to him, 'Well done, good and trustworthy slave; you have been trustworthy in a few things, I will put you in charge of many things; enter into the joy of your master.' And the one with the two talents also came forward, saying, 'Master, you handed over to me two talents; see, I have made two more talents.' His master said to him, 'Well done, good and trustworthy slave; you have been trustworthy in a few things, I will put you in charge of many things; enter into the joy of your master.' Then the one who had received the one talent also came forward, saying, 'Master, I knew that you were a harsh man, reaping where you did not sow, and gathering where you did not scatter seed; so I was afraid, and

I went and hid your talent in the ground. Here you have what is yours.' But his master replied, 'You wicked and lazy slave! You knew, did you, that I reap where I did not sow, and gather where I did not scatter? Then you ought to have invested my money with the bankers, and on my return I would have received what was my own with interest. So take the talent from him, and give it to the one with the ten talents. For to all those who have, more will be given, and they will have an abundance; but from those who have nothing, even what they have will be taken away. As for this worthless slave, throw him into the outer darkness, where there will be weeping and gnashing of teeth.'"

n the first section of this book we looked at the structure of the office: boss, team, and direct reports. Then we considered some of the challenging aspects: annoying colleagues, open plan, and the office gossip. Finally we looked at three key events in the life of the office relating to arrivals and departures: the new recruit, getting the sack (P45/pink slip), and retirement. In each case we looked to see where God might – unexpectedly – be in those. In the second section we looked at dilemmas in the workplace and considered the opportunities they might present to work with God in the healing of creation. In both sections we called upon Scripture to help us understand how God might be present in those people, events, and things. In this final section, however, I want to turn that around and start with a passage of Scripture – a single parable – and, in its unpacking, see what it might begin to tell us about the workplace. But the passage, the parable, I have chosen is a controversial one...

In fact, there are few other parables in the Gospels that inspire one group of people and repel another group with as much intensity as the parable of the talents. On the one side, for some it is an inspirational, validating story of what it means to work hard with what we have – our talents – and make something of ourselves. For others it's an almost unique biblical affirmation of the necessity and rewards of hard work. Again, for others it's a clear endorsement of the profit motive. For still others it's a realistic parable based on the observable fact that some people have more gifts and skills – or capacity for hard work – than others or, put differently, that we are not all equal, and wishing that we were will not make it so.

On the other side, however, for some it is an inexplicable, almost inexcusable affirmation of some, or all, of the above. Inequality, the profit motive, the punishment of the unsuccessful: what is there that's Christian in this parable, they ask? It must be a mistake, either of the traditional interpretation or, even more likely, a later story slipped into the Gospel not based on anything Jesus said or taught, by an author suborned by the rich and powerful to represent their views. From the already privileged senior slave to the harsh master, many feel this parable simply doesn't fit with the incarnational reality of the God of love.

I am not going to come down on one side or the other of those arguments – at least not yet. But in our quest to find out where God might be in our everyday lives and, in particular, where or how He might be present in our workplace, the parable is particularly fertile ground. There is the first and most obvious point that the story of the parable is the story of people at work, entrusted with vast sums of money and expected to use them in commercial ways. This is, right on its face, a story about workers and work. People are given assignments, they have responsibilities, and they have to report back to the boss, who then assesses them and rewards them with further work responsibility – or punishes them with demotion (or the sack). The relationships are business relationships. There is one worker who obviously has real commercial smarts, another who is not quite as high-powered but still does pretty well, and then there is the one who has no commercial savvy at all, and who lets his employer's money sit in the ground doing nothing. So we have the successful risk-taker and the conservative, risk-averse colleague who'd much rather do nothing than try anything. And there's a hierarchy. It really is just like a workplace.

So the form of the parable lends itself to our enquiry as to how God might be present in the workplace. But additionally, when the parable is read in a metaphorical rather than literal way, it may offer other insights into the workplace. The inequality that seems to lie at the heart of the parable – in terms of skills, in terms of responsibility entrusted, in terms of outcomes – is an issue faced every day. We need to examine where God might be in that. And, slightly differently, there's the question of hierarchy – at the very least between the master and his slaves but possibly also between the slaves themselves. Whether literal or metaphorical, where is God in that?

In this third section, I want us to delve into the perspectives on the workplace that this parable may offer by looking at all four of the characters involved: the master and those whom I'll call the five talent slave, the two talent slave, and the one talent slave. In separate chapters we'll try to look at the workplace through their eyes, and then stand in the workplace and look at them. We'll examine how each of them feels in the workplace, and where, if anywhere, they may perceive God as being present. But we'll also look from the workplace at how, sometimes literally, sometimes metaphorically, what they represent affects the workplace. Before we get on to the characters, however, there's one other key participant that we will spend some time looking at in this chapter, and that's the talents themselves. But before even that, some words of context on the parable as a whole may be helpful.

The parable sits in Matthew 25 among a series of parables dealing with the Parousia or second coming. It is immediately preceded by the parable of the wise and foolish virgins, some of whom were waiting prepared, their lamps full of oil, for the bridegroom at the wedding whenever he might appear – and the others who were not and were shut out of the wedding banquet. And before that story, there is the parable of the faithful and the wicked slaves, one of whom was working when the master unexpectedly returned, the other of whom was abusing his fellow slaves and drinking with sinners. So, contextually, and on one level, the parable is about preparing properly, effectively, for the second coming and the time of judgment. It's about living our lives right, and fully, in expectation of the return of Jesus which can happen at any time. It's about how we do the work of the Lord, while the Lord is still away, knowing that He will return. But, this being a parable, it can operate on several levels. So while we shouldn't forget this central context, nor should we be blind to imaginative applications of the parable on other levels.

Let's now turn to the "talents". There is an immediate problem with the meaning of the word. In English and American usage "talent" has come to mean "skill or ability". Therefore, on a straightforward reading of the parable using this meaning, God is here handing out skills and ability, and then giving still more to those who already have. The poet John Milton, in his famous sonnet on his own blindness, helped shape this particular meaning:

When I consider how my light is spent
Ere half my days in this dark world and wide,
And that one talent which is death to hide
Lodg'd with me useless...

It's literal and it's powerful. But while we can read the parable in this way, new possibilities are opened up if we can get away from that English meaning and return to its meaning in Jesus' time. The word talent, rather like the word pound, was a measure of weight, which also became a measure of money. Originally about 60 pounds of silver, it equated in Jesus' time to about 6,000 denarii. Bearing in mind that one denarius was the average daily wage, a talent was about sixteen years' worth of wages. In other words just one was a substantial sum of money, five was enormous, and eleven was astronomical. I'll come back to the size in a moment, but let's just note a few other things important for our consideration of the workplace which may flow from the talent being a sum of money, rather than a skill or gift.

First, this is not, therefore, necessarily directly a story about God-given abilities, but rather a story about the entrustment of something of great price to various individuals. We are told, of course, that the slaves are given different amounts of money according to their ability. But this is not necessarily a parable about using our own skills and gifts in our own service.

Second, the sums of money – the talents – are something given, entrusted by the master when he leaves and required to be turned back over when he returns (even if he then re-entrusts them to certain of the slaves). So, again, the parable is not directly about innate talents which cannot be disentangled from who we are. It is rather about something entrusted to us, which we are expected to work with – fruitfully – and then return to the person who gave it to us.

Third, it is unclear in a metaphorical reading what the talents are. But they are clearly somehow connected with the kingdom of God. Is it personal salvation and awareness? Is it helping others? Is it bringing other people to faith? Is it living a virtuous and faith-centred life that inspires others to do the same? Is it about the healing of creation? We simply don't know – it may be one, or a combination, or other things. But what is clear is that it is important to the master, and he intended the talents entrusted to the slaves to be used and grown in the service of the kingdom.

Then there is the size. If one talent is sixteen years' wages, five is eighty years' worth. That's a lot to entrust to a slave. Once we accept that these talents were money, rather than skills, the size is important because of those to whom they were given. Slaves, those way down the pecking order, were here entrusted with huge wealth. The master didn't entrust the talents to his fellow owners or to his friends, but to his slaves. In that sense (and we'll examine this in another chapter) this parable is more about equality, at least of opportunity, than it is about inequality. Slaves, if they can handle it, are as worthy of being trusted as the leaders of society.

One other thing I want to mention before turning more directly to possible implications for the workplace is how the talents are actually used by the slaves. Once again, we are not told how they were used to make more talents other than by "trading" (and the one talent slave being criticized for not even putting his one talent on deposit with the bankers to earn some interest). What is clear, however, is that they are something capable of being put at risk, and capable of being lost as well as multiplied. But despite this risk, and despite their enormous value, the talents exist to be used, not to be wrapped in cotton wool. However the parable is read, the talents must be used to make more talents.

So, finally, what might the talents themselves in this parable reveal to us about how God might be present in the workplace? Well, the first obvious, but nevertheless contentious, point is that this parable on its face – literally – does endorse commercial activity and, more specifically, the using of money to make more money. To be sure, in its metaphorical sense, the parable is about exploiting gifts entrusted to us by God, until the time when He comes again. But we shouldn't completely dismiss the literal story. Jesus was not in the habit of using stories about bad actions to point people in the right direction. So, while not everything has a direct read-across – for example the apparent harshness of the master – we can take some things from it. And one of those is that while this is perhaps not the full-throated advocacy of the profit motive that some of its supporters might like to claim, Jesus does indicate that – in the right settings – using money to make money is completely acceptable. So, perhaps the most obvious application of this parable to the workplace lies in its potential to address the widespread mistrust in the church of both profit-making commercial activities as well as money itself. Like it or not, this is a parable that upholds commercial activity – even, I'm afraid, banking. For Christians in the workplace that is welcoming and affirming.

Of course, I should add that the parable doesn't tell us that money is good, or that we will be doing God's work if we earn more talents for Him by any means we wish as long as we end up increasing the amount. We'll look at the motivation and actions of both master and slaves in subsequent chapters, but suffice it to say here that the talents themselves are – as is all money – essentially neutral. It is what we do with those talents that makes them good or bad. But in this parable the talents, and their increase by two of the slaves, are held out as a good thing. And that does indicate that in the right context commercial activities in the workplace can be good. In other words, done well, done properly, these activities will validly contribute to the building up of the kingdom. As a result we must be open to the possibility that God has placed them there for us to use in this way. If we approach the workplace with the idea, the preconception, that good cannot possibly be achieved there, then the chances are that it won't be. But if, in part thanks to this parable, we are open to the possibility that God can work through instruments such as money and in the workplace, then who knows what might happen? As we said in the first chapter of this book, God can turn up and do amazing things in the most unlikely places.

Let me finish on a personal note. This has always been a parable that has driven me, haunted me almost. For many years – my ambitious youth and beyond – I took it as an injunction, a commandment, to strive as hard as I could to make full use of my God-given gifts. To fail to make the most of them was a sin for which, in some way, I would pay the price. That obviously was based on Milton's meaning of "talent" in the parable – but also, of course, on the needs of my own personality. I had found the parable that I needed to motivate me, to drive me in the way that I wanted to be driven. In middle age, and with a better understanding of what the "talents" in this parable really are, I still see this parable as one of the most important biblical passages for me. There is still some of the "drivenness", the feeling that I will be held to account if I don't nurture and grow the talents. But importantly – very importantly – this is modified by a new understanding that this is not about me and my skills and abilities, but about a gift entrusted to me by God which I have been asked to look after and grow. As I said earlier, it's hard to know what the gift is, but I know it has something to do with the kingdom and something to do with helping God's people, about the healing of creation, which at the end will be perfected. Because the "talent" is something external to me, the parable is no longer about me and what I can make of myself. It's no longer simply a personal, motivational tool. Rather, because the talent is a gift from God, at some stage to be handed back to God, then it must be used for God's purposes. So, instead of an inward-looking focus, I realize that the parable is outward looking. This is still "my" parable, but, at last, it has also become God's parable – it's not all about me. What it is all about is this: that we frail humans have been entrusted with something of great worth, as fellow workers with God in his kingdom. That truly is a gift.

22

The Five Talent Slave

Matthew 25:14–16, 19–21, 28–29 (NRSV)

[Jesus said] "For it is as if a man, going on a journey, summoned his slaves and entrusted his property to them; to one he gave five talents, to another two, to another one, to each according to his ability. Then he went away. The one who had received the five talents went off at once and traded with them, and made five more talents… After a long time the master of those slaves came and settled accounts with them. Then the one who had received the five talents came forward, bringing five more talents, saying, 'Master, you handed over to me five talents; see, I have made five more talents.' His master said to him, 'Well done, good and trustworthy slave; you have been trustworthy in a few things, I will put you in charge of many things; enter into the joy of your master'… So take the talent from him, and give it to the one with the ten talents. For to all those who have, more will be given, and they will have an abundance…

As we noted in the previous chapter, the parable of the talents is loved by some and loathed by others in equal measure. But of the four characters in the parable, it is often the slave with five talents who elicits the most emotion. To some he is the paragon of hard-working achievement, the role model making the very most of what he had. To others he is the true (bad) proto-capitalist, concerned only about increasing what he already has and then getting still more from the poorest of the slaves. But to get behind these emotional responses we need to look harder at the parable.

We start with the five talent slave, examining how he feels in the workplace and where, if anywhere, he may perceive God as being present. And then we'll look from the workplace at how what the five talent slave represents may affect the workplace.

So let's try to stand in the shoes of that slave. Over the course of this story what does he feel, and where might he see God? Of course, we're short of many of the facts we need for any sort of psychological profile, but on the other hand the story is rich enough to give us hints. Here is a smart, successful, slave. Three "S's", each of which is worth a little time. While, as I said, this parable is more about developing God's gifts than developing our own, we are also told that the talents, the sums of money, are distributed to the slaves according to their ability. So we know this slave is the smartest of the three. But in this story it's not enough to be smart; you've got to be successful, too. And he is – very successful. He takes this vast sum of money – 300 pounds of silver, about 80 years' worth of the average daily wage – and he doubles it. That's an impressive performance; in business-speak, a great return on equity, especially for a slave. And that's the third "S". This man is neither a rich landowner nor a wealthy merchant, nor an educated scribe, nor a Pharisee. He's a slave. It's not just that the talents don't belong to him. He doesn't belong to himself. He's a good, a chattel, owned by his master. Three "S's" which make this an unusual story.

So let's look at each of the "S's" through his eyes. First, "smart". Because of what he does in the course of the story, we can assume that the five talent slave knows that he is smart. Indeed that and his success are two things that the people who don't like this parable hold against him. He has a gift, they say, and he then gets more. But put yourself in his shoes for a second.

I don't know how many of you reading this are eldest children, but I am, and I know the weight of expectation that goes with that – not just from parents and grandparents, but from many others. An expectation that can begin to seem like a duty: to carry forward the success of the next generation. Sometimes in small things, sometimes in large – but expectation, pressure. And that's what this slave has: pressure, pressure to succeed, to meet expectations, to meet the numbers. So his ability, his skill, his smartness, does not come without challenges. He gets given this vast sum of money, with consequently higher expectations of him than of the other slaves, and he's told to make something with it. A mixed blessing, perhaps.

And that second "S": successful. He is successful. We don't know how he did it – although I think we're allowed to assume that he did it in a "good" way. Didn't rob a bank, steal from old grannies, or sell securitized sub-prime mortgages. No, our man went out, and through skill, through his smarts, turned 300 pounds of silver, about 135 kilos, into 600 pounds of silver. Under pressure of expectation – and quite possibly also under pressure knowing about his master's moods and reputation – he performed spectacularly.

But then there's also that third "S": slave. And this is significant for two reasons. The first interlinks with the second "S" of successful. As we've already said, this was not the rich merchant, or landowner, or scribe whom we might expect to be successful. This was a slave. And that makes the success more extraordinary. Some claim that Matthew exaggerated the amount of money the slaves were entrusted with, and that the story in Luke, which instead refers to ten pounds – not nothing, but not a king's ransom either – is closer to the original. But while the amount in Matthew makes the achievement even more impressive, at the heart of it is the fact that this is achieved by a slave. He was surrounded on all sides not just by thieves and robbers, con artists, snake oil salesmen – all the usual commercial dangers in other words – but also by wealthy free men who could use the law against him to legally steal from him. He was surrounded by people who could use their networks of business contacts against him. In the face of all this, our slave doesn't just preserve his master's capital, doesn't just earn a healthy 10 per cent return. He knocks the ball out of the park – 100 per cent! By him – a good, a chattel, property owned by someone else. It's a remarkable achievement.

But that's also the rub of this, and the second significant point about him being a slave. He's owned by someone else. With now 200-plus years of fighting for the abolition of slavery, the very concept seems intolerable to us. This man uses his smarts, he's successful, and yet not just his profit, but also his very ability, legally belong to someone else. It's pure exploitation. So does our man feel aggrieved? Chafing under the yoke of oppression? We obviously don't know, but there are signals that he does not. We're told he went straight out and started trading with them. He put everything into doubling the talents. He didn't sit back and just concentrate on preserving capital. He didn't even work just until he'd made a decent return. He went for the big one and made it. That's not the action of a disgruntled employee – or a scared one. He made the big bet, and won big.

So here's how he may have seen it: not as exploitation but as opportunity. If we turn this upside down, change the angle to look at it, he's not someone being ruthlessly exploited but someone being lavishly trusted. Someone – his master – thinks he's good enough to be trusted with a huge sum of money. Trusted to go out, without micromanagement or even supervision, and not just keep the capital intact but grow it as extravagantly as he can. Here's a man whom the world sees as a non-person – a good, a thing – and someone trusts him enough to pull him out of a place where a good job for a slave would be keeping the books or watching the wine cellar. It's an amazing affirmation of this man's ability, his skills, his character, that the master trusts him in this way. Sure, it comes with some pressure, probably some anxiety, but you can tell from the way that the five talent slave reports back to the master that he realizes – and relishes – the opportunity that has been given to him.

So what might the five talent slave tell us about where God can be in the workplace? How might his story reveal the possibilities of God there? It is true that we can view the workplace as a place of oppression and exploitation. Even jokingly, we can refer to ourselves as "wage-slaves". But we can also view it as a place of opportunity. That is going to be easier if our boss offers us the big opportunities on a plate, but we can also work to create those. And, like the parable, in the workplace there is the opportunity to work with someone else's resources to create something meaningful. So, whether it's in a sales team or in the chance to create a brand new function, that opportunity is scary and there is pressure. But it can be fulfilling, not just because of the opportunities that it offers, but for the trust, the confidence of someone else that it manifests. The metaphorical meaning of the parable relates to God entrusting us with the responsibility not just to work in, but also to help grow, His kingdom, until He returns again. But we can marry that metaphorical reading with the literal story to come up with another possibility. We talked in an earlier chapter about how humans can find their fullest expression through working with the Spirit to discover their vocation in the workplace. And it is through Spirit-led work that we can become God's co-workers in the workplace building something – whether a product or a service – which will become part of the creation to be perfected at the last day.

So what the five talent slave may tell us is that in making work more productive, in increasing output, we are also growing and healing God's creation. Now this comes with all my earlier caveats and provisos about the nature of the business, the way the work is done, and other features of the workplace such as fairness and diversity. But if those are met, then God can be there in the workplace in those opportunities – commercial opportunities – offering us the possibility to work for Him growing the kingdom. Looked at in this way, we can again echo Jacob after his dream: "Surely the Lord is in this place – and I did not know it!"

So that's the parable, carried over to the workplace through the eyes of the five talent slave. Smart, successful, and a slave, he is given the scope to use his smarts, and to be successful, and to get past being a slave. He is trusted and succeeds. Similar opportunities may be offered to us in the workplace, and those may equally be godly possibilities. But we also said that we would switch around, and look from the workplace at him, to see how the five talent slave affects it. Obviously there is his success. That can and should be inspirational to others. I'll deal with the praise which ends with "enter into your master's joy" when we look at the two talent slave, but I want to deal here with what many regard as one of the most objectionable bits of the parable – the reward of the extra talent taken from the one talent slave.

This seems unfair and punitive. Worse than that, it seems like the rich get richer. Envy, already perhaps an issue because of the five talent slave's initial success, will only be magnified. How can that be good for the workplace? Well, we'll deal with the one-talent slave in much more detail in another chapter, but I would argue that at least one of the reasons why that talent gets given to the five talent slave is because it's clear that he will be able to make something of it. This is not necessarily the story of a first-century banker's bonus where the rich guy just gets richer because the game is rigged. In fact, our insight that the talents never belong to him, are simply entrusted to him, here means the master who invites him to "enter into his master's joy" also invites him to take on even greater responsibility. So not a bigger bonus, not a chance to buy the latest Ferrari, but a chance to do more work, using more of the company's resources, to grow the company even more. Looked at in that way, the reassignment of the talent is for the good of all who depend on the company, the business – not just the master and not just the five talent slave.

And here the workplace can actually help us understand the parable. As many of you will know from experience, there are few things worse for the morale of the team than someone who is incapable of carrying out their job. The task inevitably falls on others in addition to their own jobs, and no one is happy. Things go much better if the work is re-assigned to someone who can do it properly so that the whole enterprise works better. Looked at in that way, the reassignment of the talent is actually good for the business as whole, not any one individual.

So the five talent slave is *smart, successful*, and a *slave*. He is not some uber-capitalist, however, or a Master of the Universe. He is someone who has come from nothing – who owns nothing – and, trusted by his master, he has repaid that trust. Yes, he has more skill and ability than either of his two fellow slaves. But that doesn't make him better; it means that more is expected of him. So in this parable – ostensibly about commercial success and failure – what the five talent slave might be telling us about God in the workplace is this: that to be offered the chance to grow something, to be offered the trust to do that, may be an opportunity to participate as a co-worker with God in growing His kingdom and healing

His creation. That won't apply to every job and won't apply to every method of doing every job. But wild success in the workplace, using our skills to extravagantly grow production of, for example, medical equipment, or mid-market financing, or IT services, really can be working with God to double the talents. Certainly, we must be careful, we must keep our eyes open, and we mustn't trample on others to achieve it. But if we do it well – even to the extent of picking up work that others can't perform – then we will be serving our fellow workers, all those who depend on that business, and also our God and His creation.

23

The Two Talent Slave

Matthew 25:14–17, 19, 22–23 (NRSV)

"For it is as if a man, going on a journey, summoned his slaves and entrusted his property to them; to one he gave five talents, to another two, to another one, to each according to his ability. Then he went away. The one who had received the five talents went off at once and traded with them, and made five more talents. In the same way, the one who had the two talents made two more talents... After a long time the master of those slaves came and settled accounts with them... the one with the two talents also came forward, saying, 'Master, you handed over to me two talents; see, I have made two more talents.' His master said to him, 'Well done, good and trustworthy slave; you have been trustworthy in a few things, I will put you in charge of many things; enter into the joy of your master.'"

In the previous chapter, to try to explain some of the pressure under which the slave who was handed five talents by his master might have felt, I compared him to being an oldest child: that heavy weight of expectations – some external, some self-imposed – that can follow from being first in the birth order. The five talent slave knew he was the smartest, knew he had been given the largest amount of money, and knew that the most was expected from him. He was the trailblazer, but he also potentially had the furthest to fall.

In this chapter we turn to look at the slave handed two talents by his master. So again, we'll first try to stand in his shoes. To return to the theme of birth order, if the five talent slave was the oldest child, then perhaps the two talent slave is the middle child. I am not a middle child, but my middle daughter is quick to tell me how difficult it is! You are always measured against your older sibling. Everything that they do is new and unique, but you trail afterwards, treading where they have trodden, without the appreciative "oohs" and "aahs" of parents and grandparents. You're always measured against that older sibling and have to try to surpass them at everything. But, of course, you can't, because even if they did it worse, they still did it first. At the same time, neither are you the last child, the pampered younger one (although not in this parable). Being middle child – I am firmly told – is a raw deal.

So here we have the two talent slave. He's not the smartest and he's not the dumbest. He's right in the middle of the pack. He does better than the one talent slave but not nearly as well as the five talent slave. He's not called up first by his master, and so where the five talent slave hands back ten talents and then gets one more, the two talent slave hands back four and gets no bonus. We live in a world where we worship the winner. Being number one is often all that counts. Gold gets everything: the endorsements, the national anthem, the ticker tape parade, the television interviews. Silver gets a medal and a bunch of flowers. There's the best, and then there's the rest.

Is that how it turns out in the parable? Well, not exactly. In fact, the two talent slave shows not an ounce of resentment. He acts in exactly the same way as the five talent slave. We're told that the moment the master entrusts him with the money he goes out in the same way – with alacrity – and makes two more. He doesn't drag his feet; he gets on with it. As we said of the five talent slave in the previous chapter, the two talent slave is also smart, successful, and a slave. In absolute terms he's not as successful, but in relative terms equally successful. And when called to account by his master he doesn't grumble or moan that he was only given two talents to trade with and could have made more. He proudly presents back his two talents in words identical to that of the five talent slave: "Master, you handed over to me two talents; see, I have made two more talents." What is most telling in this story, however, is not how the slave behaves but how his master behaves towards him. He treats him – with the exception of the extra talent – no differently from the five talent slave. The latter turned 300 pounds of silver into 600 pounds, the former turned 120 pounds into 240, but the master treats them both the same. He greets the two talent slave in the same way as he does the five talent slave: "Well done, good and trustworthy slave; you have been trustworthy in a few things, I will put you in charge of many things; enter into the joy of your master."

So what does this have to say about how the two talent slave might perceive God to be present in his workplace – the place where he has doubled his talents? Well, before getting to that we have to remind ourselves again of the context of the parable. This is one of a series of parables in Matthew's Gospel that deals with the second coming and being prepared for that. In this story – bearing in mind that context – all of the slaves are given gifts by God, gifts that in some way relate to growing the kingdom of heaven, to spreading the word of God. And they are judged in terms of their participation in growing the kingdom. In this context the two talent slave is treated exactly the same way as the five talent slave. The point is that he has done the best he could and is as worthy as the five talent slave. The master praises him, expands his area of responsibility, and "welcomes him into his master's joy". For the two talent slave this very definitely is not the middle child scenario. Rather, even if he is not as smart as the five talent slave, even if he doesn't make as much money, he has fulfilled his potential just as much as the other slave has done. What he may see of God in this parable, therefore, is not a judge of absolutes but a judge of relatives. Not a respecter of status, or total amounts, but someone who sees through that to how each individual human being – as different and diverse as we are – achieves the best he can, by working with his God to the fullest of his abilities.

On this reading, therefore, what is important is how we make the most of what we have. So that flips this parable from being about an unfair God who unequally distributes skills and talents (and, by implication, rewards), and it turns it into being about a God who respects each human being's uniqueness, those quirks of nature and genetic mixing, and who rejoices whenever one of us does the very best that we – we, not someone else, not the "perfect" person – can do. That is true equality. Not an absolute winner-takes-it-all outcome, but rather praise, and love, and joy for each and any of us who makes the best of what we have.

So, as with the five talent slave, how might the story of the two talent slave help us find God in the workplace? One of the ways relates to opportunity. The workplace should not be somewhere that is dominated by a single superstar, but a place where everyone can – according to their abilities applied to the opportunities offered to them – be a "winner" by doing the best they can for the business. And as co-workers with God in healing His creation, God is not looking for a single big winner. He's looking for a team – the biggest possible team – to help Him. As Jesus says elsewhere, the harvest is plentiful and the labourers are few. God is not looking for a few winners to shower all the glory on. He wants as many winners as possible.

At this this point, however, I need to make a couple of

important qualifications. When these chapters were originally being delivered as talks, several people asked me – worried after the first few – how we, as Christians, especially at St Martin-in-the-Fields with its tradition of outreach to the homeless, could spend so much time talking about the winners, and apparently praising them, when there's a huge loser in the one talent slave, and a cruel boss in the form of the master. I'm going to come to those characters in the final two chapters, but I want to emphasize that my purpose in looking at this parable is to see where God might be in the workplace – even a commercial workplace. I believe passionately that God is interested in His entire creation, not just the obviously good and holy bits. This parable covers the full spectrum of activity that one can see in a workplace from spectacular success to devastating failure. God does not – let me emphasize this – God does not hate or despise a loser. But neither, I also believe, does God automatically hate or despise a winner.

But again that needs qualification. Neither am I preaching the "Gospel of Prosperity". This is not about a God who especially loves winners, nor about a God who shows His blessings and favour to His chosen ones through material, earthly prosperity. This is not about a world where what we do using our own skills and efforts makes God love us and reward us with more and more talents. These two slaves – people as I've said before who do not even own themselves – are entrusted with a gift that never belongs to them, and which must be returned to God. Furthermore, although not quite as explicit in this parable, they do not achieve what they achieve through their human efforts. They achieve what they achieve because they are working for God, with the talents entrusted to them. This is not about independent human achievement; it is about what we can achieve when we are working for God – working with the word of God, to heal, to build up

His kingdom. This is not about a big bonus or the new sports car; it's about participating in the ongoing act of creation, in building the kingdom. And that is not about material success.

As we've seen, the "talents" are never defined. I believe that in the workplace setting, the talents may refer to building better medical equipment that helps more people, or increasing crop yields to feed more people, or building more houses for a growing population – that also is part of the kingdom, part of the healing of creation. But going beyond the business of the business, I also believe the talents can refer to using other opportunities in the workplace – ones we've also mentioned before: the opportunity to help the person in the cubicle next to you, the opportunity to make the team work better and more harmoniously, the opportunity to help your company interact with the local community. Those are all talents – things of great worth – that we can help God by growing. So the parable is literally about vast sums of money, but, read with the imagination that I believe Jesus intended, it can cover every other gift, every other opportunity offered by God in the workplace. This parable should not be read as supporting a gospel of material things. But, at the same time, it is absolutely our calling as Christians to live God's gospel in the material world.

So, after those necessary qualifications, let's turn briefly to look at the two talent slave from the standpoint of the workplace. How does his treatment make the rest of us feel, and what might that tell us about God? Well, part of this is exactly what we have been talking about from the other side when looking at it through the slave's eyes. The fact that there can be more than one winner can encourage everybody in the workplace to do as well as they can, rather than giving up in despair because they feel they'll never be the best. The fact that the master treats the five and two talent slaves almost identically, giving them more responsibility and inviting them both to enter into his "joy", as he puts it, points out that while the physical rewards may be different, the appreciation of the master, the boss, is not.

To truly understand this, however, we do have to put aside our normal human way of measuring ourselves – by money. In so many ways money has become the main, often the sole, measure of our worth at work: "He or she earns more than I do, so they must be *valued* more." The very terms, the very words we use, such as "value", reinforce that measure. But this parable tells us something different. Yes, the different slaves get entrusted with different amounts, but the love in which they are held is equal, the reward they get – still more of their master's lavish trust, his confidence – is the same. They are both asked to share in his joy in equal measure – not with one getting five units of joy and the other getting only two units, but the same.

So carry this across to the workplace to see what it might tell us about where God could be found. It's not just that everyone can be a winner if they do the best they can do, but also that the reason why everyone can be a winner is because money – although central to the literal story – is not the real measure of worth in the parable. It is the estimation, the trust, the confidence in which our fellow human beings hold us that matters (the master in this story, but in our world also our peers and those who work for us). So again, this parable which seems to be about measuring skills and rewarding them with money is actually about something very different, where the true reward is the sharing of joy.

I want to finish by going back to the middle child theme for a moment. Despite what I've just said, you may still instinctively feel that the obviously smarter, more successful colleague, sibling, friend will cast a long psychological shadow.

You may recall in the first chapter of this section that I owned up to some element of "drivenness" that is spoken to by this parable. But, to take my life as a lawyer, for example, I know that while I'm not the worst lawyer around, nor am I the best. Not anywhere near it. But I do work with someone who I think is. Someone once asked me what it was like working with him. I'd never really thought about it in those terms, but the act of formulating the answer made me realize why being the two talent slave is not a bad thing. "Once I admitted to myself," I eventually replied, "that he's ten times cleverer than I am, my life became much easier." I could admire him for who, and what, he was without worry (or for that matter envy) that I was not as good as him. Instead, I was freed to be as good as I could be doing what I did, rather than trying to be as good as he was doing what he did. It was a real liberation. I'm fairly certain that he gets paid more than I do, and probably gets more recognition, but I don't care. I do what I enjoy doing, and do it as well as I can. In turn, the trust placed in me by my boss is as great as the trust placed in my colleague. It's a liberation that allows us both to work for a common goal, rather than competing against each other.

The two talent slave is a successful member of a successful team. If we can make the most of what we've got, working for God, maximizing the things entrusted to us – even in a commercial undertaking – then we shouldn't be jealous or worried that we haven't been given five talents. We should be thrilled we've been given two, and all the opportunity that goes with that.

24
The One Talent Slave

Matthew 25:14–19, 24–30 (NRSV)

"For it is as if a man, going on a journey, summoned his slaves and entrusted his property to them; to one he gave five talents, to another two, to another one, to each according to his ability. Then he went away. The one who had received the five talents went off at once and traded with them, and made five more talents... But the one who had received the one talent went off and dug a hole in the ground and hid his master's money. After a long time the master of those slaves came and settled accounts with them... Then the one who had received the one talent also came forward, saying, 'Master, I knew that you were a harsh man, reaping where you did not sow, and gathering where you did not scatter seed; so I was afraid, and I went and hid your talent in the ground. Here you have what is yours.' But his master replied, 'You wicked and lazy slave! You knew, did you, that I reap where I did not sow, and gather where I did not scatter? Then you ought to have invested my money with the bankers, and on my return I would have received what was my own with interest. So take the talent from him, and give it to the one with the ten talents. For to all those who have, more will be given, and they will have an abundance; but from those who have nothing, even what they have will be taken away. As for this worthless slave, throw him into the outer darkness, where there will be weeping and gnashing of teeth.'"

n the two previous chapters, we've looked at the slaves who received five talents and two talents, and examined what they might be able to tell us about God in the workplace – a God who can be present in commercial activity, and who can make us co-workers with Him in that activity. Well, that may be fine for those two, but what happens when we turn to the one talent slave? It doesn't seem fair, or just, or right, that he's treated like that. Why is the one with the least ability the one who is punished the most? If this is to be read as an allegory of capitalism, some listeners to the original talks told me, then this story illuminates in a particularly vivid way the underbelly of the beast. The rich get richer and the poor get poorer. It says it right there in the parable: "For to all those who have, more will be given, and they will have an abundance; but from those who have nothing, even what they have will be taken away."

So, as I said in the first chapter of this section, there are those who regard this parable as a later, post-Jesus addition to the Gospel or, at the very least, as words of Jesus, maybe, but ones that have been seriously rearranged and manipulated. One commentator, referring to another version of this story in a biblical writing now lost, suggests that the five talent slave who, in that version, squandered the money, was actually the slave who was cast out; that the one talent slave, who eschewed trading and profit, was welcomed into the master's joy; and the two talent slave was merely rebuked for being moderately successful. That seems to me to be a rather hard sell, at least in terms of the two mainstream Gospel readings, so I think that even if we dislike it, we have to take our story as we find it – but then see what we can make of it.

To help address the issues surrounding the one talent slave, I want to remind you quickly of a couple of things we've already talked about and then introduce something new. Remember that in Jesus' day, "talent" referred to a huge sum of money. So this parable is not about God handing out skills. It is a story about the entrustment of gifts, which must be returned at some stage. To be very clear, this is not a story about a slave disadvantaged by God (or by the master) from the beginning and then punished still further for being the runt of the litter. Any judgment here is based on the use and stewardship of the money, the talents, entrusted to him.

Second, the metaphorical thrust of the story is about whether people are prepared for the Parousia. This is not about how well each one does personally in the exercise of their innate skills. It's about how they live their lives in anticipation of an arrival which is inevitable, but whose time is completely unknown. So again, as used by Matthew, the Gospel writer, this is not a story about the little guy getting pushed into the gutter by the fat cats. It's about who's prepared for the kingdom – and who's not.

Both of those points we've covered before, but here's something slightly new. Before the Gospel writer gathered this and its accompanying parables into a section of the Gospel dealing with the second coming, they were almost certainly used by Jesus in a slightly different way: as what some writers call "challenge parables". In relation to the second coming, the Gospel writers had a problem. Jesus had not returned to earth as quickly as they anticipated, so they had to find ways to keep the faithful, faithful. Part of that was by explaining the wait as a test – a what-did-you-do-while-waiting-for-Jesus test – and as a time for beginning to build the kingdom on earth. But in fact, Jesus himself may originally have had another purpose. His aim was to make people aware of the mess they were in right now, of the state that the people of Israel found themselves in – still in exile, and still so far from God. And who had helped to get them there? Their leaders: the scribes and Pharisees, the religious establishment. They had taken the promise of the living God and turned it into a dead letter. Extravagant, hierarchical, with minutely detailed rules governing this, that, and the other, the leadership of the Jewish nation had squeezed the life out of the word of God and replaced it with a human construct. As the generations passed, keeping the food laws, all the observances, and the rituals of worship became the obsession of the leadership – justice and mercy, and the God-oriented teachings of the prophets were forgotten or misrepresented. On this reading, therefore, it has been suggested that the one talent slave in fact represents the scribes and Pharisees. Given the talent – the word of God, the ability to grow the kingdom of God – they play it safe. They try to preserve what they have been entrusted with exactly as it is. They take no risk, they bury it in the ground, so that they can hand back exactly what they were given – nothing more and nothing less.

They don't see the word of God as something which can be grown, as something which can be used in a positive, active way to make more good things, to heal creation. It's more like an heirloom – a precious, beautiful object – which they must preserve but not alter in any way. And the reason for this is that they have misunderstood the nature of God. They truly believe that God is simply a God of judgment and a God of punishment – a God who will think less of them if they don't play it safe and keep all the forms and outward structures of the Law of Moses intact down to the last word. Their obsession with the Sabbath, or the food laws, or the honour due to them because of their obvious "goodness", has got in the way of what God really means. These leaders have been handed this gift, this opportunity to work with God, and they've just wrapped it in a cloth and buried it in the ground. That was why Jesus challenged them. (And that was why they killed Him.)

So, on this reading the one talent slave emerges in a new

light. He is no longer the disadvantaged little guy who gets screwed for playing it safe. No longer the little fish that gets swallowed up by the big ones. And no longer, perhaps, the victim of his rapacious master. If the one talent slave had made one more, he would have been treated exactly the same, even though the most successful slave would have handed back ten talents, and he only two. So this is a story not about only one winner, with everyone else a loser. It's about making the best of what you have. If this is a challenge parable, then the leaders of Israel have been given an opportunity which they miss, a challenge to which they fail to rise.

But, some of you may be asking, why are these leaders being cast as the one talent slave, rather than the five talent slave? Wouldn't it be better if the five talent slave had failed, and the one talent slave succeeded? The triumph of the little guy? Well, possibly, but in context Jesus might also have been saying that the people with the most ability to grow the kingdom were not the leaders of Israel – perhaps they were the prophets or other non-establishment figures (think of the Good Samaritan) – and that even then, the leaders of Israel, although entrusted with only one talent, still managed to mess up. We don't know, but I firmly believe that this is not a parable about the weak getting trampled on.

So let's carry this across to the workplace. This is now not about the least talented person in the workplace, the guy on the lowest rung of the ladder, who gets crushed under the heel of the others. This is part of a challenge – a challenge about people put in positions of responsibility, and opportunity, who fail to make the most of what has been given to them. Let me try to give a workplace example. Perhaps we're talking about the personnel department, about HR. The five talent slave might be the head of HR, responsible for bringing on and nurturing the top leadership of the business. The two talent slave might be the person responsible for the middle managers of the business – not the big strategic thinkers at the top of the organization, but the operational leaders who make sure that things actually happen and who are, perhaps, the next generation of leaders. And then the one talent slave is responsible for new recruits, for integrating them into the organization, for getting them the right training, for finding them mentors, and for reassuring them as they settle in. These people are not the leaders of tomorrow, but they may be the leaders of the day after tomorrow. The one talent slave is not entrusted with things that are of greatest value now, but things which may be in the future if properly nurtured. His "talent", the new recruits, are as critical to the business as the others, because they both do the basic work now, in the short term, and also hold the promise of the future.

If the one talent slave plays it by the rule book, however, sticks to the guidelines, does nothing more, then he will have failed; he'll have misplaced the trust put in him. His job is not just to make sure the new recruits get through the day. His job is to ensure that they grow, that they blossom and flourish in this new environment, that their inventiveness and enthusiasm are channelled into productive ends. If the one talent slave just views his job as keeping himself and the new recruits out of trouble, then nothing will really have gone wrong. It's just that neither will anything have really gone right. An opportunity to build, to create, that may not come around again may have been missed. Through conservatism, through fear, through being risk-averse, the one talent slave will have held people back to their detriment and to the cost of the organization. If he had been brilliant with the new recruits, the CEO of the company – the master in our story – would undoubtedly have valued him and loved him as much as his more senior colleagues. He would have been the best that he could be. But he wasn't, and so, at least in our story, he had to go.

Now let's switch that round and look at the slave from the perspective of the workplace. If this were just about the weakest getting trampled on or scapegoated, the effect on morale could be horrible. Everyone would wonder, "Is it me next?" And there is also the way that the master deals with the slave, and the language he uses – but again we'll come back to that in the final chapter. So let's just stand in the workplace and look at the one talent slave. What do we see? Well, remember first that this is not about the guy on the lowest rung of the ladder getting the boot for doing a menial job which others think unimportant. This is about someone who has had some trust placed in them – quite possibly considerable trust – and he's not lived up to that. Let's go back to our reimagining of the parable. It may not be that he's failed to double his pot of cash. Perhaps, it is, as we've just heard, that he's failed in his basic HR job of allowing others to reach their full potential. Or perhaps it's something else that has caused some small but vital function in the workplace to stagnate, with a knock-on effect on bigger things and more people. Perhaps he was asked to sort an HR issue out but he didn't – so it's got no worse, but also no better, and everything's on hold.

Or, reimagining this slightly differently again, maybe burying the talent is the equivalent of doing the bare minimum: in not a second before 9.00 a.m., and out not a second after 5.00 p.m. Scrupulously observing her employment contract but doing nothing extra – not putting her shoulder to the wheel with everyone else during busy periods, not picking up the slack when someone else is ill but the work still has to be done. We instinctively view the one talent slave – especially because of the English understanding of the word "talent" – as someone short-changed at the beginning of the story and treated shamefully ever thereafter. But Jesus tells these stories for a reason and He challenges us, and our imagination, to find out what that might be. So here, if the one talent slave is, essentially, a free-rider, let's rethink it, and ask if her removal from the office, the workplace, may actually make things better for everyone else.

I want to finish this chapter with another personal story, which looks at this from yet another angle. For the past couple of years I've taught a class on God in the workplace for people getting ordained. I talk about vocations and about where God might be in the workplace, and how He wants us to work for Him there. And, at some point, I inevitably get what I call the "Tesco question" (after the UK supermarket chain). How, someone asks, can you talk about God being in the workplace, and someone working for the kingdom and finding fulfilment in that work, when the work itself is stacking shelves at Tesco? Those who ask that seem convinced they've posed an unanswerable question, something that must exclude the possibility of most modern commercial workplaces being meaningful parts of the kingdom. But putting aside the potential pastoral insensitivity, the question really needs turning around. I am no apologist for the excesses of capitalism, but if God can meet Jacob in the middle of nowhere, put down a ladder from heaven and transform his life, then I think I owe it to God to exercise my imagination and keep my eyes open in unlikely places, including at Tesco. So I always tell them a story.

My wife has an uncle who lives in a rural part of the northern US. In the sixties he was countercultural and never wanted to work in an office or a factory, so he lived on the family farm. When kids came along, he realized he needed health insurance, so he went to the local supermarket and signed on to stack shelves for the hours necessary to get coverage. He's now been doing that for decades. He does it well. It has supported his family. The customers in the store know him, and he brings a smile to their faces. Many people might think that he hankers to be a two talent or a five talent slave, but actually he doesn't. And who are we to say that being part of a chain of commerce that brings food at reasonable prices to people who perhaps don't have much cash – and also bringing a smile to their face at the same time – is not helping to build God's kingdom?

We measure success and ambition and achievement in human terms. One of the many things this parable does is challenge those measures. The one talent slave is chucked out not because he's insignificant, but because he's actually just as important as the five talent slave. However, he lets the side down. This is not about kicking the little guy when he's down. This is about a God who loves us all equally whatever our level of ability, and wants us all to help Him by doing whatever we can do. It's about a God who invites us to work with Him not to achieve the impossible – but simply the very best we can. That is the challenge God gives us. That is the challenge of the parable of the talents.

25

The Master

Matthew 25:21, 22, 26–30 (NRSV)

"His master said to him [the five talent slave], 'Well done, good and trustworthy slave; you have been trustworthy in a few things, I will put you in charge of many things; enter into the joy of your master'… His master said to him [the two talent slave], 'Well done, good and trustworthy slave; you have been trustworthy in a few things, I will put you in charge of many things; enter into the joy of your master'… But his [the one talent slave's] master replied, 'You wicked and lazy slave! You knew, did you, that I reap where I did not sow, and gather where I did not scatter? Then you ought to have invested my money with the bankers, and on my return I would have received what was my own with interest. So take the talent from him, and give it to the one with the ten talents. For to all those who have, more will be given, and they will have an abundance; but from those who have nothing, even what they have will be taken away. As for this worthless slave, throw him into the outer darkness, where there will be weeping and gnashing of teeth.'"

And so, at last, we get to the master. We've examined all the other actors in the story, and we now come to the hardest, both literally and metaphorically: hard in spirit, apparently, and certainly hard to defend. Condemned from his own mouth, he has everything that is unattractive about the strict moralizing father, about the heartless slaveowner, about the hard-charging modern CEO. It's all about maximizing profit. Nothing else counts. And for some, this also is the unattractive Christian God. The God who is used to justify oppression. The God who demands more than He ever gives. The God who deals a rough hand to some and then seems to relish punishing them further.

We've talked before about whether this parable is really about the God of love. How can we square the master here, many ask, with, for example, the father in the parable of the Prodigal Son? There the father forgives and celebrates; here the master judges and condemns. There the son has wasted half his father's wealth and is still welcomed in; here the slave hands the wealth back intact and is still thrown out. There the other son who has faithfully and modestly served his father for little reward seems implicitly criticized; here the slaves who make huge profits get all the praise. What's going on?

Well, let's step back a moment and revisit the context of the parable of the talents one final time. As we have discussed, this parable is about being prepared for the return of Jesus, and how we work for the kingdom, for the healing of creation – the job entrusted to us as "talents" in the parable. So in this story, on that reading, the returning master would logically be Jesus. But while serving Jesus may not always exactly be a walk in the park, nor does our Saviour, who died on the cross to save us, "reap where [he does] not sow, and gather where [he does] not scatter". So perhaps Jesus isn't the "master" and we need to look at this a little harder.

In the preceding chapter we also introduced the idea that Jesus may have originally used this as a "challenge parable", rather than the Parousia parable it subsequently became. Under this reading the one talent slave is, perhaps, the leadership of the Jewish people, failing in its task to bring that people back to God. So on this reading, perhaps the master is God the

Father, Yahweh. Certainly there are some characteristics in the description of the master that might seem to echo the Old Testament God who could punish His own chosen people by opening fissures in the ground to swallow them up, sending plagues to destroy thousands upon thousands of them, and even driving them into exile from the land He had given them. But again, remember that it is God the Son who tells the story. The Son, again, who died for us, the Son who entered into a New Covenant with us that is based on His sacrifice and His love. So again, it doesn't quite seem to work to equate the master with God the Father. God the Father, no more than the Son, reaps where He does not sow, and gathers where He does not scatter. We need to look at this a little harder to figure out what is really going on.

So what might be happening here? Well, we can, of course, argue as an initial matter that this is simply exaggeration. The Father, or Jesus, was, to be sure, cross/annoyed/disappointed at the one talent slave, but the bit about taking the talent away and casting him out is a little hyperbole just to make the point. But go back to the Prodigal Son to see why, at least in my view, that doesn't work. We like that story, but if it is to have real force we can't take the Bible, and especially the words of Jesus, and read as truth the bits we like, while seeking to explain away anything we don't – even if for the best of motives. Certainly, in the Anglican/Episcopalian tradition we have to read the Scripture anew in every generation applying our reason, although with deference to tradition, to determine how God might be speaking to us through the word. But applying our reason to the Bible is a little different from amending or excising the bits we don't like.

So, how do we read this parable to tease out what might be going on with the master? One way may be to approach this as a lawyer (my other job) or a policeman might approach a statement made by a witness. What is said, and what is not said?

- The first description of the master has him leaving and entrusting vast sums of money to the three slaves.

- The next thing we hear about him is he returns and asks for an accounting.

- After that, when the five talent slave reports back with ten talents, he re-entrusts all those talents to him, praises him generously, and invites him to enter into the master's joy.

- Then he does and says exactly the same for the two talent slave.

So at this point in the story, over halfway through, we have a master who entrusts huge amounts of money to the slaves and lets them get on with using it. And we have a master who praises and raises to equality with himself two *slaves* who have done what he asks of them. If we stopped the story here, we would have a very different view of the master. It is only after we have learnt these things that we get to the one talent slave and the description of the master as a harsh man. But I think it's very important to note where this description comes from. It comes from the one talent slave, not from the master. That is that slave's perception of the master, and it is one not articulated elsewhere.

Wait a moment, you say, the master acknowledges all this. But let's look again – does he? What he actually does is to repeat the words back to the one talent slave. So what we need to do is find his tone of voice. You can, of course, because of the assumptions we bring to this story, quite easily hear a snarl in what the master says. But if you listen to it differently, might you not also hear frustration in it, or possibly sarcasm? "Oh you knew that did you, and even then you didn't do anything? According to you I'm apparently a hard man, and not even that stirred you to move outside your comfort zone? You're useless. Get out!"

Imagine for a moment: what if one of the facts we don't know is that the master sat the slaves down before he left and told them, even explained to them, how to go out and trade? As we said in the previous chapter, the one talent slave has had something of value entrusted to him and has failed to deliver. He has been given a message which he chooses to ignore. It is entirely possible that the master who rewards the two slaves who have done what he asks of them (and more) is loving and generous, but that the one talent slave – whether the leadership of Israel, or someone who has failed to build the kingdom before the second coming – drives him to distraction and he loses his temper. If we look at it from a slightly different angle, perhaps what we see is the one talent slave trying to put the blame back on the master – the one who trusted him, remember, with a considerable sum of money – and make it all into the master's fault. Inconceivable, you think? Maybe. But how often do we shirk our duty, our obligations, run away from what we know we ought to do, by saying that there was never any point in trying because we knew we had been set up to fail? Better to play it safe and blame someone else for having raised the bar too high in the first place.

So let's go back again to the Prodigal Son for a moment and revisit those contrasts we noted at the beginning. There the father celebrates – but actually here, with two of the slaves, the master also celebrates. There the son wastes the money; here it's handed back intact. Yes, *but*. The key difference is, quite obviously, in the attitudes of the son and the one talent slave. The returning son realizes he's messed up and comes back to beg forgiveness. He's returning to the fold. He's a soul reclaimed. In our case, there is no repentance – in fact, nothing like it. There's more a shifty, defensive attempt by the one talent slave to move the blame. What the master may be saying is "I didn't have to entrust that talent to you. You knew what had to be done and took that talent from me. But then you did nothing – other than to tell me when I got home that it was my own stupid fault for trusting you." The father/master/God figure in these two parables is presented with two very different cases, potentially calling for two very different responses. The one talent slave wasn't asking for forgiveness or admitting to fault. He was trying to shift the blame for not doing what he ought to have done.

Now let's carry that across to the workplace, and I'll give a personal example. Back in my law firm days, I remember working for people who did get very cross with me about the work I did for them. There were among those people ones who definitely reaped where they did not sow, and gathered where they did not scatter – hard men. But others were not. They heaped on praise when it was deserved but were not so much hard as, rather, disappointed when I didn't reward their trust. And that would happen when, for example, too scared to admit I hadn't understood the assignment the first time, I didn't go back for clarification but simply did the assignment wrongly.

I remember standing one day outside the door of a partner who had given me a project (and whom I really respected) and hearing him complain to someone else – without knowing that I was standing there – about the work that I'd done. I was mortified. I should have asked for more clarification, for help. But I didn't, I hadn't, and so I'd wasted his time as well as mine because of a fear that was created by me, not him. I had accepted the task and then failed to perform it. He had every right to be cross.

But then something happened. After first sneaking silently away in embarrassment and shame, I then went back to the partner and admitted what I'd done (and not done). I admitted my fault – *my* fault, mark you, not his – and didn't try to blame it on him. And the story changed. It somehow switched from the parable of the talents to that of the Prodigal Son. I was given another chance. And that's an important point about the parable of the talents. There is nothing here that precludes repentance and forgiveness, other than the attitude of the one talent slave. Effectively, he hurts himself – as, differently, does the brother of the retuning Prodigal Son – by getting trapped inside himself. He cannot see that what the master has offered him is an opportunity – whether it is to grow money or to grow the kingdom. He sees only the downside, only risk. But he does it to himself. Succeed, and he will be loved; fail, and he will also be loved – if he accepts that love. But shift the blame, hide behind excuses, not face up to it... that's when the trouble comes.

So, to look at this again from another, slightly different angle, there can be a kindness in being reproved by someone. If we have a habit, or an attitude, or a fault, that prevents us from reaching our full potential, is it really kinder to let us continue to make the same mistake again and again and again, or is it actually kinder to set us right, in order to allow us to reach our full potential? The language of the end of the parable is harsh. There's no doubt about that. Whether as a Parousia parable or a challenge parable, Jesus wants to make clear what's at stake: the redemption of the people of Israel and/or participation in eternal life. That's not something always to be discussed in moderate tones. The words themselves cannot, should not, be carried over literally into the workplace environment. But I think the concepts can. If you prove yourself worthy of trust at work, you will be given more. If you're not up to it, however, then that responsibility will have to be taken away and given to someone who can do the job properly. And if you truly struggle with every aspect of your job and consistently cannot fulfil the expectations of the role, then you may have to leave the business. In an earlier chapter, I mentioned Jack Welch, the former GE boss, and his management principle of removing the bottom 10 per cent. It didn't work quite like that; it wasn't that harsh in practice. But the principle that it harms not just the business but also the people themselves to have them in jobs they cannot do, may, if acted on appropriately (I do emphasize appropriately), express not cruelty, but actually turn out to be a kindness.

I want to finish with a more general thought, and that is how we tend to view people two-dimensionally. We see the master as a harsh man in part because that's how we expect to see him. But this is also the master who trusts, praises, and loves the two other slaves. Because that doesn't seem to mesh with the subsequent treatment of the final slave, we dismiss it. But we shouldn't, because together they give us a more complex, more accurate picture of the master. A generous man, but also a man with a temper. A trusting man, but one with high expectations. A loving man, but a demanding one. It fills out the picture. And might we not also say that of God? Loving, caring, forgiving, trusting, but also expectant, challenging, and occasionally frustrated by the messes into which we get ourselves and others? If we face up to our faults, admit those mess-ups, and try to do better the next time, then He's right there, standing next to us, cheering us on, ready to help us in so many ways. But if we mess up and then try to blame Him, what we really do is cut ourselves off from Him and from all of those good things He offers us.

To remind you one final time, the parable of the talents

is not about the unequal handing out of skills and about the punishment of the weak. It is about whether we try to be the best that we can be, working with God to build His kingdom, heal His creation, including in the workplace – which, like everything else, will be perfected at the end of time. It's about being ourselves, not trying to be people we're not. It's about doing only what we are capable of doing, but doing it very well. It's about a God who entrusts us with things of enormous worth – the possibilities of being His co-workers – and who will love us for what we have done unless (and only unless) we hide the gift, don't ask Him for help using it, and then turn round and tell Him it was all His own fault anyway. Our God loves us. He really does. And all we have to do is love Him back.

A Personal Reflection on Witnessing at Work

Matthew 28:16–20 (NIV)

Then the eleven disciples went to Galilee, to the mountain where Jesus had told them to go. When they saw him, they worshipped him; but some doubted. Then Jesus came to them and said, "All authority in heaven and on earth has been given to me. Therefore go and make disciples of all nations, baptizing them in the name of the Father and of the Son and of the Holy Spirit, and teaching them to obey everything I have commanded you. And surely I am with you always, to the very end of the age."

I should be totally honest and start by saying that the Great Commission – rather like the subject of prayer – makes me feel totally inadequate as a Christian. The mere thought of going to work and "mak[ing] disciples of all nations" brings me out in in rash. At the beginning of *Thank God it's Monday*, Mark Greene tells a wonderful story about how leaving a half-cooked chicken in the fridge of what he thought was an empty office led to the opportunity to spend an hour talking about God with the head of Ogilvy & Mather, the worldwide advertising agency. I always have two reactions to this story: first, immense admiration for Mark; and, second, terrible guilt over whether I'd have even gone into the office to get my chicken, far less brought up the subject of God with the CEO. Despite having written an entire book about how God can be in the workplace, and how He cares for and loves it, and how it is a place where we can be His co-workers in ongoing creation, the thought of "witnessing" to that message in the workplace fills me with complete dread.

But why? Perhaps it's because I'm an introvert (surprisingly common among clergy), and public witnessing seems such an extroverted activity. But that's not quite enough. My "day job" involves considerable amounts of public speaking, and I enjoy preaching. (Besides which, I know most of the people at my work quite well.) Perhaps it also has something to do with the secular nature of today's workplace. Religion just seems totally out of context, something that doesn't belong – even rather weird. But perhaps that's not sufficient either, because we spend plenty of time at work talking about all sorts of things – some of which are pretty esoteric. Perhaps, to get a little closer to the bone, might it be because I have a sneaking (if only occasional) feeling that whatever the theory, God may not be present in *my* workplace – perhaps because of the nature of my work – and so talking about Him there is, at best, naïve, at worst, misleading.

Well, all of the above probably play some part, but, in the end – for me at least – the real problem with the Great Commission comes down to a single word: "make". "Therefore go and *make* disciples of all the nations..." To my post-modernist (and post-imperial) ears, the implication of compulsion sounds all wrong. In part, I don't want to be made or compelled to do anything, so why would I compel others? But also, especially in this context, it seems the very opposite of what I (we) should be striving for: people willingly, but completely freely, coming to Christ.

So do these last words of Jesus in the Gospel set me (us)

up for failure, set us up to live with guilt and inadequacy? Well, they shouldn't. But to prevent that we need to do two things. First, we do need to escape from what seems to be the literal straightjacket of the word "make". And, second, we also need rescuing from the idea that the Great Commission is a simple numbers game about new converts. We have a stereotype of fervent witnessing at revivalist meetings; or men (almost always) with megaphones and sandwich boards on busy streets; or of the "body count" of the converted at the end of a mission. All of those have their place, but witnessing – although, as you can tell from the first paragraph, I constantly regress on this – is actually much broader, often more generous, more affirming, and, in many ways, much more surprising than we might think.

So, at this point, having started to broaden the subject out, I could lay out a logical (if rather dry) exposition of four theories of witnessing, and examine the pros and cons of each. But in witnessing, we are actually telling the story of our own faith, as well as the story of the faith, so it might be better if I just recount some personal stories instead. Two relate to my ordination; one to my ongoing experience in the workplace.

In the first story, my then boss's deputy, a devout Roman Catholic, followed my progress towards ordination warmly and closely. After the big day, he asked innocently enough for a photo or two. There was one amazing one (nothing to do with me, everything to do with St Paul's Cathedral, and episcopal robes, and golden light, and the photographer's skill), so I overcame my slight misgivings and shared it with him. The next thing I knew, he had sent it to approximately 200 of my colleagues! That was not something I would have done myself (see above) and I was, to put it mildly, a little apprehensive about their reactions.

Over the following few weeks, I went on several foreign trips. And to my utter surprise, a number of my colleagues asked how I felt about my job now that I was ordained. Did I ever worry? Was there anything about it that seemed ambiguous? Yes, both, I replied. And a number of them told me how glad they were to hear that; how they had imagined they had been alone. Did I explicitly mention my faith? No. Did I make disciples of them? I doubt it. But did they ask me questions that allowed me to give them answers that reassured them in their doubts, and comforted them that they could be good people in an ambiguous place? Yes. And did they ask me those questions because I was ordained, perhaps because they'd seen a photo? Yes. It certainly doesn't sound like the Great Commission, but is it "witnessing"? Perhaps. Simply to be a public Christian, especially in a workplace that many view as a grey zone, to stand alongside people and share their doubts (rather than lecture them), may be Christian witness. That may not be how some understand the word, but the Jesus who dined with sinners and tax collectors (and, to be clear, priest or not, I'm in the sinners/ tax collectors category) might disagree.

The second ordination story relates to some of the conversations we had in the office where I worked at the time. In that relatively small department there was a Muslim woman, a Hindu man, an Orthodox Jew, a moderate Anglican, a committed Catholic, and a lapsed, but very enquiring, Episcopalian. The discussions we had about my motives for becoming a priest, about what it meant to me, were an opportunity to have – in a totally non-threatening way for others – a conversation about my faith journey and about what that faith meant to me. I do believe that Jesus Christ is the incarnation of the Living God, and that He came to save us from our sins. I do believe that we get the most from that gift of redemption, from our relationship with God, if we see that clearly. But I am also absolutely certain that as Christians we have a monopoly neither on knowledge nor on virtue. So we can learn from people of other faiths, and, perhaps even more importantly, people of other faiths (and those who profess no faith at all) can carry out the work of God. Being with them, talking about my own faith, and building them up to do God's work (even outside the Christian "wrapper") is part of what we are called to do. Did I "make disciples of all the nations"? Absolutely not. Did I through sharing my story with others advance the kingdom even a little bit? I hope so. Witnessing? Perhaps.

My last story (which is really less a story than a composite of experiences over several years) relates to what we do for other people in the workplace: how we support them, how we help them, and how sometimes we simply just stand with them in their darkness. Before going any further, I need to make very clear that I am no saint (neither in my actions nor in reserves of patience) and also that time constraints often mean that I have to pass by, leaving opportunities to help lying on the side of the road. In short, I'm a pretty normal, very fallible human being. But, occasionally, where I can, I try to help – bereavements, family problems, concerns about work. In several earlier chapters we looked at the parable of the sheep and the goats and the metaphorically starving, imprisoned, and naked in that place. It's important to note that doing these things doesn't earn us special heavenly brownie points – we are simply fulfilling our basic obligations as Christians. But it is also important to recognize that when undertaking these obligations in the workplace to help those in need, we can also be witnessing.

For it to be that, however, we do also need to find some way to be explicit about the fact that we are inspired by our Christian faith. That can be very gentle, but if we are (in St Teresa's words) God's arms and feet on earth, acting out in practical ways God's love for those in need, then we should not be ashamed to make that clear. As Christians we believe that while healing can start through actions, it will only reach its fullness when the source and nature of the gift is fully understood – when we realize what it is God has given us, and the burdens that He takes away from us. And this is why – with this gentle witnessing – the workplace is such an important mission field. When we sit alongside people for large parts of every week – people who experience, like us, all of life's sorrows as well as its joys – the opportunities to help are almost endless. To turn this to witnessing doesn't require a sermon, or a theological exposition, or a dramatic gesture, or a special sign – it simply requires us to find some quiet way to show where we're coming from, and why we are the way we are.

So, as I hope these stories show, if we define the word a little more generously, then those of you like me who feel nervous (or, more honestly, inadequate) about "witnessing", will in fact realize that you can witness in many ways. But – as always – there are also a couple of words of warning, especially if the witnessing involves explicitly talking about God. When you do that you almost always move the conversation to a more intense level. The effects on others can be dramatic and unexpected. So, even if you're being gentle (or think you are) please always consider the effect on the other person:

- Some people in the workplace are highly vulnerable, and some people there may have been damaged by the church (perhaps they have felt condemned, or shut out, or even were sexually abused by clergy). It requires pastoral sensitivity to (re)acquaint such people with the God of love.

- You also need to be very aware of the power of relationships in the workplace, particularly if you hold a position in a hierarchy. It can be difficult to hold separate the role of inviting people to faith, and the role of running a secular structure in which you control (or play a part in) other people's careers. People should not feel that their success or failure in the office depends upon them adopting your views.

- You should always be very careful about directly bringing your faith into business arguments and decisions. There is a theological "Caesar's coin" aspect to this, but, just as important, many of your colleagues will view it as, at best, your attempt to short-cut any argument by an appeal to a higher power, and, at worst, as you looking down on them, judging them. "What Would Jesus Do?" can be a very appropriate question to ask yourself as you try to make your own mind up on a business issue. However, asking your colleagues that question when making a business decision may turn out to be not only an ineffective, but, in fact, a negative way of witnessing.

- And, of course, you must respect the rules of the workplace, even if they seem petty and mean-spirited. I wrote in an earlier chapter about the wearing of crosses. That can be a form of witnessing (or at least an adjunct to it), but if it is forbidden, then you should not storm out claiming persecution. I believe a much more effective way of witnessing to our faith is to accept that decision and make clear that our faith is even stronger for it, as is our commitment to the workplace and our fellow employees.

To reiterate: we can and should witness at work. We can do it through words, and we can do it through actions which, nevertheless, we link visibly to our faith. But, however we do it, we should always do it sensitively, and usually very gently. Because in the end we must remember that witnessing is not about us. It's not about how good we sound, or how many people we bring to Christ. The purpose of witnessing is so that others also get the chance to make the journey that we are on; so that they also can begin to see the gift that we have glimpsed; so that they, too, can begin to understand that their sins have been forgiven. If we assume it is about us, however, and that it is primarily our salvation (or higher place in heaven) that is at stake, then we are more likely to approach witnessing as guilty failures, or overly zealous advocates. And neither advances the gospel.

So, we come back to the Great Commission. I firmly believe that Jesus was not telling His apostles then, and is not telling us now, to force (or guilt) people into belief. Rather, He wants us to be messengers – to encourage, to facilitate, the discipleship of others for what it does for them. To tell of how a burden of sin is lifted, and relationships – real, life-enhancing relationships – are restored with both God and other humans. But just in case we are still attracted to (or made to feel inadequate by) that word "make", consider this: the all-powerful God who created the world could click His fingers today, wipe clean our minds, and "make" us all into contented disciples (or automatons). But He has chosen not to do that; He has instead given us a choice. He wants us as willing, joyful, and sentient partners in His ongoing work of creation – but through our choice, not through heavenly or earthly compulsion. And yet He yearns for as many of those free, but willing, disciples as possible – so the workplace with its vast, if underappreciated, potential is a vital mission space. That is why witnessing there – unpleasant though the word may sometimes sound, scary though the prospect may often seem, and enormously careful and sensitive though we must always be – is a fundamental part of being a Christian. Because the good news we have heard is far, far too important not to be shared with the whole world.

Suggested Questions for Study Groups

These questions try to touch on several of the issues raised in each chapter. They are far from comprehensive, and groups should not hesitate to add or subtract. In particular, some groups may wish to consider questions more specifically considering the Scripture reading for that chapter and/or questions more directly related to the involvement of God in that area or issue. Others may wish to focus more on secular structure and process issues. Either is fine! But the questions below are often intended to be provocative – including in questioning some of my own views – because it is only by asking hard questions of ourselves that we can start to strip away the human narrative (illusions, rationalizations) we have built around our lives at work, and begin to discern where God might be and what He might want of us.

Part I: Where is God at Work?

1. The Workplace

- Do you feel that "God" and "workplace" are opposites?
- Does your church empower and encourage you as a worker?
- Can you see anything of God in your workplace?

- How does the story of Jacob's ladder speak to you of the unexpectedness of God?

- Do you see the potential for any of the possibilities listed in this chapter in your workplace?

2. *Your Boss*

- What is it about the word "obey" that we find so difficult?

- Have any of your bosses inspired you? If so, how?

- Do you see a place for different (and clearly delineated) roles and responsibilities in a workplace?

- Do you understand the creation story as (on any level) a story about work?

- Does it help you to understand yourself as a co-worker with God in an ongoing creation story?

3. *Your Direct Report*

- Do you have levels of hierarchy in your workplace? How do you feel about that?

- Do you have people who report to you? Do you feel responsible for more than just their work product? If so, how do you feel about that?

- Can you think of bosses who have set examples that you have followed – both positive and negative?

- Do you feel your job calls upon (or fulfils) your "natural" gifts? If so, in exercising them do you have any sense of working with God?

- Do you think about your business more broadly than the goods it makes or services it provides?

4. The Team

- Have you ever felt part of a true team at work? If so, how did that differ from a collection of individuals who are labelled a "team"?

- Can successful teams have different (but complementary) personalities, or does it work better if everyone is the same?

- What can the disciples tell us about teamwork both before and after the resurrection? Can this tell us anything useful for today's workplace?

- Have you ever understood your co-worker to be your "neighbour"?

- Do you ever feel that God can work through you – either helping others or in the work you do?

5. The Office Gossip

- Do you ever gossip? How does it feel?

- Have you ever been gossiped about? If so, what do you think about the "sticks and stones" saying?

- How do you feel as the listener – the recipient of gossip?

- Does gossip affect the atmosphere in your workplace?

- Is there a practical (non-judgmental, non-preachy) way to promote "positive gossip"?

6. Open Plan

- Do you work in an open plan? If so, do you like it? If you don't like it, why not?

- If you do, do you see any of the work-related advantages (greater cooperation, teamwork, etc.) actually occurring?

- What about the possibilities it might present for helping your co-workers?

- If you work in an office (four walls and a door) do you feel cut off or part of the team? What if the team you lead works in open plan and you don't?

- How do you feel when a good idea is stretched beyond its useful boundaries by a desire for profit maximization?

7. The Annoying Colleague

- Do you have annoying colleagues? How do they annoy you?

- Has it ever occurred to you that you might be the annoying colleague?

- If you were to raise a challenge in the workplace, how would you do it without being "annoying"?

- If you were Peter how would you feel about Paul after being attacked by him in Antioch?

- Do you feel "annoyingness" may come mostly from not understanding or knowing the "annoying" person?

8. The New Arrival

- When was the last time you were a new arrival in a workplace? Did you feel that sense of freshness?

- If you have been in your workplace for some time, do you feel challenged by new arrivals?

- Can you see the advantages to the team in a mix of more established workers and more recent arrivals?

- Do you worry about the future, or are you able to enjoy the present? If the latter, how?

- Does refreshment from handing your cares about tomorrow to God sound practical or simply pious?

9. Retirement

- Do you eagerly anticipate or do you dread retirement?

- If retirement concerns you, why? Is it because you enjoy work, because you need money, because of loss of status, or because you need something to fill your time?

- Is your workplace rigid or flexible about retirement? What are the pros and cons of each?

- Do you think "full" retirement may be ungodly, or does that sound like the Protestant work ethic taken to its extreme?

- Have you ever worked in a workplace with people in their seventies and eighties? Did it add or detract from a) the effectiveness and b) the atmosphere of the workplace?

10. The P45 (or "Pink Slip")

- Have you ever been sacked? How did you feel then? And later?

- Was there anything beneficial in that for you either in the short term or in the long term?

- How do you feel about people in jobs to which they are not suited? Has that ever been you?

- Have you ever had to fire anyone? How did that affect you?

- Does the story of Job help – or just make you wonder why God can allow these sorts of things to happen?

Part II: Where is God at Work in Work's Dilemmas?

11. What Happens If... I Face an Ethical Dilemma at Work?

- Do you ever see God in the dilemmas and the difficult choices you have to make in the workplace?

- Do you regard the solutions to these dilemmas and choices as involving "ethics"? If so, do they also involve "Christian ethics"?

- Does the end ever justify the means in the workplace, or are both always important?

- Do you feel that how we deal with small decisions day-in and day-out in the workplace is important, or is it really only the big ethical decisions that matter?

- How would you take an ethical stand in the workplace explicitly to persuade/encourage/include your non-churchgoing (and/or non-Christian) colleagues?

12. What Happens If... I Am Asked to Do Something Against My Christian Beliefs?

- What do you think about the idea of the big and small circles? Do you agree that a small number of beliefs are "core", while a much larger number are "peripheral"?

- Can you tell when you have reached a point in an argument where someone has to lose?

- Have you ever felt your Christian beliefs under challenge in the workplace? Were they core or peripheral beliefs? What, in particular, do you think about being able to wear a cross at work?

- Are there any principles really worth fighting for?

- Can you ever conceive of having – in relation to the workplace – to take up your cross and follow Jesus? What might that mean?

13. What Happens If... I Am Told to Compete Against My Colleagues?

- Have you ever experienced destructive competition in your workplace? If so, what did it feel like?

- Can there ever really be constructive competition, or is that just a management excuse for getting people to work still harder?

- Which set of Bible passages in this chapter appeal to you more? Why?

- Can you compete against "the system" or, by definition, must competition always be against other people?

- How do you balance the downsides of competing against your fellow workers with the wish/need to be the best you can be?

14. What Happens If... My Boss Wants Me to Work Harder and Harder?

- How do you relate to the story of the fisherman?

- Over the years have you found yourself working harder and harder? Does that mean longer hours and/or more intensity and/or greater stress?

- If so, how has it affected each of those four relationships?

- Did you do it yourself (at least in part) or was it really your boss and/or circumstances that caused it to happen? If you did do it to yourself, why? Need, ambition, filling a space?

- If you do feel that you have the work/life balance right (or at least under control), how did you do that? And how do you maintain it?

15. What Happens If... Someone Has to Take the Blame?

- What is the difference between saying "I am sorry" and "I take the blame"?

- Have you ever taken the blame for something you did not do? Or not taken the blame for something that you did do?

- Do you recognize any of the "macro" or "micro" business situations described? Who should take the blame? What would you do in those circumstances?

- Do you have any sympathy with Caiaphas? If not, why not?

- Can leading by example ever work?

16. What Happens If... Everyone's Always Arguing?

- Do you like arguing? Do you find it constructive always/sometimes/never?

- If you find arguments difficult, why is that?

- How does it affect your view on arguing to think of Jesus as argumentative?

- Have you ever made "righteous" arguments? Can you see the danger of those slipping into self-righteousness?

- How do you feel about whistle-blowers? Could you be one, or do you think there is always some element of betrayal/lack of loyalty?

17. *What Happens If... I Have to Respond to a Difficult Email?*

- How do you feel about emails and other aspects of the information revolution? A positive for communications, or a negative for contemplation?

- Have you noticed the ratcheting up of "acceptable anger" in the press, on talk shows, Internet chat rooms, etc. in the past ten to twenty years? Does that worry you?

- What does anger do to you?

- Do you ever let the sun go down on your anger? If so, why?

- What do you think about a list of rules to help you reply? And by not replying, or replying differently, can you see any potential for "building up"?

18. *What Happens If... My Boss Asks Me to Lie?*

- Do you think you would always refuse if your boss asked you to lie?

- Do you recognize the situation that C. S. Lewis is talking about – a series of imperceptible moral shadings that carry you over the line?

- Is lying ever justified and/or acceptable? Do a) the hypotheticals and b) the Old Testament stories persuade you?

- Do you ever tell lies that hurt only yourself? Are those as bad as lies that hurt other people?

- Can we ever really be as "wise as serpents" while also remaining as "innocent as doves"? Do the examples of how to deal with the boss who asks us to lie meet both criteria?

19. What Happens If... I'm Tempted to Do Something Bad in the Workplace?

- What are the real temptations in the workplace? Are they power, hierarchy, and money? Not all of those? Or more? What about personal honesty and sexual temptation?

- Do you think that God really does give us the strength to withstand temptation?

- Do you think that "thou shalt not" is a safer way of dealing with temptation, rather than trying to subvert it?

- Can you think of times in your working life when any of these three temptations has posed a serious challenge to you? How did you react? What was the outcome?

- Are any of the suggestions for subverting temptation helpful, or do they not address practical issues (e.g. being short of money)?

20. What Happens If... I Do Something Bad in the Workplace?

- Do you carry with you those things done and things not done that attach to your personality like the barnacles on the rock?

- Does 'fessing up to God, to others, and to ourselves really sound like the answer? Or do you feel at some level that sin can only be forgiven after punishment?

- What does it mean (big question!) that Jesus died for our sins?

- Thinking back to the chapter on "taking the blame", can you see the healing benefits to the community of 'fessing up?

- Do you really accept the necessity to forgive yourself?

Part III: Where is God at Work in the Bible?

21. The Talents

- How do you feel about the parable of the talents?

- Does it alter your view if the "talent" is a sum of money, rather than innate skill or ability?

- Does it alter your view if this is seen as a parable about being prepared for the second coming?

- Do you accept that money is neutral, or is there something inherently corrupting about it – especially in very large sums?

- Does this parable speak to you in any way about an opportunity offered by God to be a co-worker with Him?

22. The Five Talent Slave

- Do you think you'd like the five talent slave in your workplace?

- Do you think that being "smart" also carries a weight of expectation, or is that the typical self-seeking statement of an eldest child/successful worker?

- Does the fact that he's a slave who owns nothing change your view of him, or the parable?

- Can you view work as an opportunity to work with someone else's resources to build or create something? Or will work always be about an unequal relationship (even exploitation) at some level?

- Metaphorically, can you see the possibilities of working with God to grow the "kingdom" like the talents were grown? How about literally, as workers with God in His ongoing creation, in its healing?

23. *The Two Talent Slave*

- Do you agree that in this parable in almost every way the two talent slave is treated as well as the five talent slave? Does that change your view of the parable?

- In your workplace are you praised for being as good as you can be, or is there a "superstar" culture?

- Do you think this parable really is about a "Gospel of Prosperity" where God materially rewards those he favours?

- Can praise ever be as good a reward as money? What about increased opportunity as a reward?

- Have you ever found comfort in admitting to yourself that while you are not "the best", you are "the best that you can be"?

24. *The One Talent Slave*

- Does viewing this as a "challenge parable" change how you feel about the story?

- Can you accept that the one talent slave was also entrusted with something precious – even if in a lesser quantity to the five talent or two talent slave?

- Have you ever worked anywhere where the junior staff were made to feel as valued as the mid-level and senior staff? If so, what did that do to the atmosphere in the workplace?

- Have you ever worked with someone who always did just the bare minimum – just enough, but never more? How did you feel about that person? What did it do to the workplace?

- How do you feel about the "Tesco question"? Can stacking shelves be working with God? If not, why not?

25. The Master

- If you just listen to the first two slaves, do you feel differently about the master?

- Even after the explanations in this chapter, do you feel there are still fundamental differences between the parable of the talents and the parable of the Prodigal Son?

- Is the one talent slave badly treated, or might he be trying to run away from his own responsibilities? If the latter, have you ever done that?

- Is the "master" in the parable God? Jesus? Does your answer make you feel uncomfortable? If so, why?

- After examining the parable of the talents from five different angles how do you feel about it? Does it tell you anything positive about the godly possibilities of the workplace?

Epilogue: A Personal Reflection on Witnessing at Work

- Does the idea of "witnessing" about your faith to others at work fill you with terror? Why? Do you identify with any of the reasons given?

- Is the Great Commission the only text about witnessing and mission? What about Luke 4:18 and John 3:16? Or, for that matter, Luke 14:23?

- Did any of the stories help broaden your understanding of "witnessing"? Can you think of additional ways to witness?

- In particular, do you think that you can "witness" through your actions to others, or is that really just trying to wriggle off the hook of full-blooded witnessing? If you believe you can also witness through your actions, then how do you make clear your faith motivation?

- Do you agree with the cautions about witnessing in the workplace? If not, why not?

Bibliography

While the literature on faith and the workplace is not very extensive, and while this book employs very few direct quotations, I am glad to acknowledge several strong influences. The debt to Mark Greene's *Thank God it's Monday* (Scripture Union 3rd ed. 2001) is clear throughout. So also that to Miroslav Volf's *Work in the Spirit* (OUP 1991), and to Richard Rohr's article "Living on the Edge of the Inside" (*Radical Grace*, April-May-June 2006, Vol. 19, No. 2.).

Other books in this area that I have found helpful (even when I ultimately disagree with some of the conclusions) include: Darrell Cosden's *The Heavenly Good of Earthly Work* (Paternoster 2006), David Miller's *God at Work* (OUP 2007), Ken Costa's *God at Work* (Continuum 2007), R. Paul Stevens' *Work Matters* (Eerdmans 2012), Ben Witherington's *Work* (Eerdmans 2011), Timothy Keller's *Every Good Endeavour* (Hodder & Stoughton 2012), Esther Reed's *Work! For God's Sake* (DLT 2010), Laura Nash and Scotty McLennan's *Church on Sunday, Work on Monday* (Jossey-Bass 2001), and Bruce Hiebert's *Good Work* (Northstone 1997). Additionally, for a short, basic, but very clear guide to some of the historical theology, it is hard to fault the Grove booklet, 94, *God at Work*, by John Goldingay and Robert Innes (1994).

On Christian Ethics, I am indebted to Sam Wells and Ben Quash's book, *Introducing Christian Ethics* (Wiley-Blackwell 2010). *Business Ethics* by Andrew Crane and Dirk Matten

(OUP 3rd ed. 2010) also helped frame some of the more specifically business issues. *Civil Economy* (Peter Lang 2007), by Luigino Bruni and Stefano Zamagni is an elegant analysis of what we have lost (but could regain) in terms of work infused with civic (community) purpose.

For the parable of the talents I relied on two older, but still higly relevant, books: C. H. Dodd's *The Parables of the Kingdom* (James Nisbet, revised ed. 1961) and Joachim Jeremias' *The Parables of Jesus* (SCM revised ed. 1963). I am also indebted to R. T. Francis' *The Gospel of Matthew* (Eerdmans 2007) – as indeed I am more gnerally to the NICNT series.

Finally, Nigel Biggar's *Behaving in Public* (Eerdmans 2011) is not about faith and work as such, but his views on how to be a Christian in a public setting speak as valuably to the workplace as they do to all other public settings.